AMAZING STORIES

THE WAR OF 1812 AGAINST THE STATES

THE WAR OF 1812 AGAINST THE STATES

Heroes of a Great Canadian Victory

HISTORY

by Jennifer Crump

PUBLISHED BY ALTITUDE PUBLISHING CANADA LTD.
1500 Railway Avenue, Canmore, Alberta T1W 1P6
www.altitudepublishing.com
1-800-957-6888

Extreme care has been taken to ensure that all information presented in
this book is accurate and up to date. Neither the author nor the
publisher can be held responsible for any errors.

Publisher	Stephen Hutchings
Associate Publisher	Kara Turner
Project Editor	Jill Foran
Editor	Pat Kozak

We acknowledge the financial support of the Government
of Canada through the Book Publishing Industry Development
Program (BPIDP) for our publishing activities.

Altitude GreenTree Program
Altitude Publishing will plant twice as many trees as were used
in the manufacturing of this product.

National Library of Canada Cataloguing in Publication Data

Crump, Jennifer
The War of 1812 Against the States / Jennifer Crump.

(Amazing stories)
Includes bibliographical references.
ISBN 1-55153-948-9

1. Canada--History--War of 1812. I. Title. II. Series:
Amazing stories (Canmore, Alta.)

FC442.C78 2003	971.03'4	C2003-904883-7

Printed and bound in Canada by Friesens
2 4 6 8 9 7 5 3 1

Cover: Detail from "The Battle of Queenston Heights," a painting by John David Kelly

To Bea Burke and the late John Alexander
Wilson, for the love of words and history
they have shared.

Contents

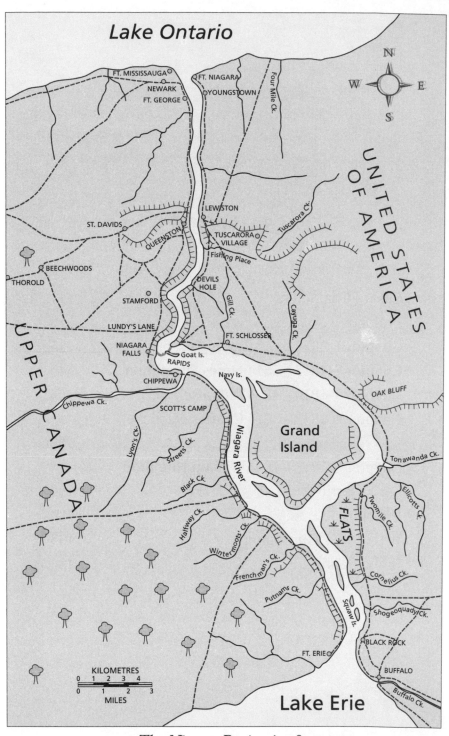

The Niagara Region in 1812

Cast of Characters

Americans
Lieutenant Colonel Charles Boerstler
Cyrenius Chapin
General Wade Hampton
Lieutenant Porter Hanks
Brigadier General William Henry Harrison
Brigadier General William Hull
Brigadier General George McClure
Colonel Winfield Scott
General Stephan Van Renasselaer
Major General James Wilkinson
Joseph Willcocks (Canadian but sided with the Americans)

British
Lieutenant-Colonel Cecil Bishopp
Major General Isaac Brock
William "Tiger" Dunlop
Lieutenant James Fitzgibbon
Lieutenant Colonel John Harvey
Lieutenant Colonel "Red George" Macdonell
Lieutenant Colonel John Macdonell, Brock's aide de camp
Sir George Prevost, the Governor General of Canada
Lieutenant Colonel Henry Proctor
Major-General Phineas Riall
General Roger Sheafe
Major General John Vincent

Canadians
Charles-Michel D'Irumberry de Salaberry
Captain Francois Ducharme
Matthew Elliott
Billy Green, the Scout
David and Jacob Manning
Captain William Hamilton Merritt
Colonel Murray
Lieutenant Frederic Roulette
Laura Secord

Native Peoples
Robert Dixon
John Norton
The Prophet
Tecumseh
Chief Walk in Water

Prologue

July 23, 1812
York Militia Barracks
Fort York, Upper Canada

Dearest Emily,
It seems ages since the Americans declared war and I had to leave you, even though it's been barely four weeks. I hate the militia. We've had to arm and clothe ourselves, the rations are meagre, and we even have to cook for ourselves! I'm desperate for home, but I have to stay. If we refuse to serve, we can be shot as traitors.
Before I left, you asked why the Americans wanted war. Well, I've got some answers for you now. There's this thing called impressment. Apparently, the British ships are stopping American ships at sea and searching them for deserters from the British army. They impress the British deserters into their navy, and they also impress Americans — thousands of them — to help fight Napoleon. I guess I don't blame them for being mad.
The boys here at the barracks say there's another reason. The Americans aim to drive the British off the continent. Some of the politicians down there believe in

something called manifest destiny. They think it's the United States' destiny to control the entire continent, including our little part of it!

Whatever the reasons are, and whoever wins, it won't really make much difference to us. What do we care if we answer to a king or a president? The crops will still be harvested, and, God willing, we'll still get married in the spring.

Anyway, the war won't last long. We are so outnumbered the Americans will beat us in no time. Although, I did hear we might have help from the Natives. One of their leaders swore vengeance against the Americans after a battle in a place called Tippecanoe, and he's persuading the tribes to join the British.

I must go now. Tell my father I'll be back to help him with the harvest whether the war is over or not.

I can't wait to see you again.

All my love,
James Williams

Chapter 1
1812
Issac Brock

F or most of the 10 years that Major
General Isaac Brock had been stationed in Canada, he had wanted
nothing more than to leave. The career soldier yearned
to be where the real action was — on the battlefields of
Europe, fighting Napoleon. But instead he was stuck in
Fort George, an old wooden fort outside the town of
Newark, Upper Canada (present day Niagara on the
Lake, Ontario), waiting for a war that might never
happen. He had sent several letters to the Prince Regent
— the head of the British armed forces — requesting
permission to return to England, but to no avail. His

boredom and frustration with life on the Niagara frontier is reflected in a letter he wrote to his brother in 1811.
"You who have passed all of your days in the bustle of
London, can scarcely conceive the uninteresting and
insipid life I am doomed to lead in this retirement."

Blonde, blue-eyed, and well over six feet tall, Brock
was a dashing figure in his scarlet uniform. At 42, he was
the commander in chief of all the troops in Upper
Canada. He had proved himself in battle and was
respected and admired by his men. He was seen as a
man with a destiny.

But could he find his destiny in the remote
colonies? Brock very much doubted it. In the early 19th
century, Canada, then known as "the Canadas," was a
loose confederacy of villages scattered along the eastern
half of the continent in two provinces, Upper Canada
and Lower Canada (present day Ontario and Quebec).
Most of the colonials were farmers, and many were
recent immigrants from the United States — loyalists
who had fled to Canada following the American War of
Independence (1775 – 1783). The fluid border drawn
after that war was still defended by a series of isolated
wooden forts, most of which were in a state of frighten-
ing disrepair. The British soldiers who manned these
forts buffered their isolation with rum and dreams of
past victories.

Sir Issac Brock

When a letter arrived from the Prince Regent in early 1812 finally granting Brock permission to return to England, he should have been ecstatic. His opportunity had arrived. Fame and glory in the fight against Napoleon could be his. But, by this time, things had become a whole lot more exciting in the colonies. Every sign pointed to war with the Americans and Brock, as the acting political administrator of Upper Canada, felt duty bound to stay. His next letter to England requested leave to remain in Canada.

Whispers of War
The colonials had whispered of war with the Americans for most of the decade, but recent rumours seemed to hold more substance. Some members of the American Congress were openly calling for war. Indeed, many of them believed that a war with Canada would barely be a war at all. Thomas Jefferson, the former American president, publicly declared that the acquisition of Canada would be, "a mere matter of marching."

And so it might have been, for the odds seemed insurmountable. America's population was seven million; it had a trained army of more than 35,000 and an ample supply of arms. By contrast, Canada's population was barely half a million; it had only 5000 British soldiers, a possible 4000 militia, and a dearth of arms.

Ostensibly, all able-bodied Canadian men could have been called up to serve on the militia, but Brock thought it prudent to arm only a mere 1500. He knew that few had any deep attachment to Britain, and fewer still could be counted on to commit to a war they saw as a fight between the British and Americans. At this time, Brock had little respect for the Canadian militia. He believed that they were ill trained and ill equipped, and that they would desert at the first opportunity. However, the general was to change his opinion about Canadian fighting men within the next few months.

WAR!
On June 19, 1812, while at a formal dinner with his American counterparts at Fort George, Brock was informed that President Madison had declared war on Canada. The officers, who had frequently socialized until then, politely finished the meal before returning to their respective headquarters to plot strategy. The whispers of war became a deafening shout as word spread. No one doubted the outcome. Canadian politicians, civilians, and the Native peoples believed an American victory was inevitable. Brock desperately needed the Native peoples as allies, but they were reluctant to back the losing side.

No one, it seemed, had counted on Isaac Brock.

"Most of the people have lost confidence," he wrote to one of his brothers. "I, however, speak loud and look big."

Brock the Bold

Isaac Brock was a natural leader with a reputation for boldness and quick thinking. His ability to bluff was legendary. In his youth, he had been challenged to a duel. He had boldly accepted, stating that he would fight the duel, but not at the usual 30 paces. Instead, he and his opponent would fire at each other over a handkerchief. His opponent had quickly backed down.

This kind of quick thinking helped Brock even the odds with the Americans before the first volley had even been fired. As soon as he heard that war had been declared, Brock passed the news on to his commander at Fort Amherstberg (now called Fort Malden, present day Amherstberg, Ontario), more than 300 kilometres away at the northwest end of Lake Erie. Shortly after Brock's courier arrived at the quiet fort on the banks of the Detroit River, the American schooner *Cuyahoga Packet* blithely sailed past on its way to Fort Detroit, Michigan. A young French Canadian lieutenant at the fort, Frederic Roulette, ordered a British captain and six sailors into a longboat. The men calmly approached the *Cuyahoga Packet*, boarded her, and told the captain and crew they were prisoners of war. The Americans were stunned — they'd had no idea that war had even been declared.

The capture of the *Cuyahoga Packet* had provided

Brock with some critical information. The boat had been carrying correspondence from William Hull, an American general who was slogging his way through the forests of western Michigan en route to Fort Detroit. Hull, it turned out, was also oblivious of his country's declaration of war.

The correspondence found on the *Cuyahoga Packet* confirmed what Brock had already suspected. Once Hull reached Fort Detroit, he would launch an attack on the village of Sandwich, near Fort Amherstberg. The correspondence also revealed that Hull felt he had greatly overestimated his enemy's strength, and that he was terrified at the prospect of fighting the Native warriors who were aligned with the British. Further, his army was small and demoralized.

Brock estimated it would take Hull at least four weeks to reach Fort Detroit, and he planned to pay him a visit there. But first he arranged to deliver a blow to the Americans on another frontier.

During the tedious years before the war, Brock had been quietly placing his men in strategic areas so they would be ready for the Americans' opening move. Now that war had been declared, he sent a missive to Robert Dixon, one of his leaders. Dixon, a Scott known as "the red-haired man," had married a Sioux woman. His loyalties were with the Native peoples who had accepted him as one of their own. He considered himself a Sioux warrior.

Dixon and his 250 warriors had already joined a group of pensioned British soldiers at St. Joseph's Island in the northern arm of Lake Huron. When they received word from Brock on July 17, the warriors and old soldiers, accompanied by a handful of fur traders, immediately followed his orders. Under cover of darkness, they silently paddled across Lake Huron to Michilimackinac Island. This island, which had been reluctantly abandoned by the British following the American War of Independence, had been crucial to the western fur trade — and would be again. After quietly waking the villagers and taking them to safety, the old soldiers, along with Dixon and his men, confronted Porter Hanks, the American commander. Terrified at the sight of the Native warriors, Hanks immediately surrendered the fort.

For Brock, it was an important moral victory, albeit a bloodless one. The British had won the first battle. It also sent a clear message to the Native peoples: the British were willing to fight and able to win. The distribution of spoils from the capture sent another message: there were rewards to be had if one sided with the British.

While his men had been achieving glory at Michilimackinac, Brock had been stuck in York (present day Toronto, Ontario), begging the politicians for arms and the authority to call up the local militia. He was desperate to be in the thick of things and was eager to be on his way to engage General Hull.

Hull had already occupied Sandwich, and Brock expected him to attack the vulnerable Fort Amherstberg at any moment. But while Brock shored up the weak defenses of Amherstberg with every spare soldier and weapon he could find, his superior, Sir George Prevost, the Governor General of Canada, was attempting to negotiate a peace. Brock was frustrated. He was afraid the war would be over before he had a chance to see action.

Finally, in early August, Brock convinced the legislature to allow him to call up the militia. Five hundred men answered the call. However, with few supplies or arms, Brock could take only half of them.

During the voyage along the length of Lake Erie, Brock and his army were caught in a storm. When the storm died, the wind died with it, and the men were forced to row their way across. Brock's own boat hit a rock. In full dress, he climbed overboard to help dislodge it. When the group was underway once again, he opened his personal stock of spirits and handed every man on board a glass. This, and similar acts of generosity, endeared Brock to his men.

Once they had landed, Brock allowed the exhausted soldiers to sleep. But the driven leader pressed on towards Fort Amherstberg. It was long past midnight when he reached his quarters at the fort. Before he had a chance to fall into bed, there was a loud knock at his door. Outside was Lieutenant Colonel John Macdonell, Brock's aide de camp. Standing next to Macdonell was a tall, lithe warrior who was promptly introduced as the Great Tecumseh, a Shawnee war chief.

Brock and Tecumseh eyed each other. Tecumseh saw a tall, broad-shouldered soldier. A soldier of intelligence and action. A leader not unlike himself. "Here is a man!" he would later exclaim to his fellow chiefs.

Brock, too, was impressed. He wrote to his brother, "A more sagacious and gallant Warrior does not, I believe, exist. He was the admiration of every one who conversed with him." The two men shook hands and Brock called a hasty war conference. While Brock's junior officers pleaded caution, Tecumseh pushed for immediate action. Brock, sensing a like mind, agreed with him.

Brock the Brash

Despite orders from his superiors to act defensively only, Brock immediately attempted to provoke a fight with General Hull. On August 15, he ordered an artillery barrage of Fort Detroit. Then he audaciously demanded that the Americans surrender. Safe within the walls of the fort with a large contingent of soldiers, Hull, not surprisingly, refused.

Later that night, after the guns had faded into silence, Brock sent Tecumseh and 500 of his Shawnee warriors across the Detroit River. Once across, they silently surrounded the fort and stayed hidden in the dense forest.

With 500 Native warriors, 700 local militia, and barely 300 regular soldiers, Brock knew his men were hopelessly outnumbered. He then used two strategies he became famous for. He ordered the British soldiers to give the militia their spare uniforms. There were not enough uniforms to go around, so they shared them — a bright red jacket here, a pair of white breeches there. On the morning of August 16, after leading this ragtag army across the river, Brock organized the men into columns and ordered them to march at twice the usual distance from one another. To the Americans watching from the fort, Brock's troops seemed twice as numerous as they really were.

Brock rode at the head of the line, his great height and red and gold uniform making him an easy target. When an aide suggested that Brock would be safer somewhere within the column, he refused. He would not, he said, ask his men to go where he was not willing to lead.

Just as the British came within range of the American guns, Brock veered off and led his men into the safety of a nearby ravine. Remembering Hull's fear of Native warriors, Brock had ordered Tecumseh to parade his troops across a field in full view of the fort immediately after the army and militia had taken refuge in the ravine. The warriors crossed the field, disappeared into the forest, and doubled back to the place where they had begun their march. Then they marched again — and again. General Hull was convinced he was facing 1500 warriors.

The terrified Hull, who had his daughter and grandson inside the fort, asked for a three-day truce. Brock gave him three hours, then frightened the hapless general even more by telling him the lie that the Native warriors "will be beyond control the moment the contest commences." Hull immediately surrendered the fort.

Brock and Tecumseh rode into the fort side by side. Brock was resplendent in his uniform, and wore a beaded sash — a gift from Tecumseh — tied around his waist. Tecumseh, in his far simpler fringed buckskin, looked equally impressive. Brock had, it is said, gifted Tecumseh with his own military sash. But Tecumseh, with a customary lack of conceit, had given it to Chief Walk in Water, a chief he considered of higher rank than himself.

Issac Brock

Brock had won another decisive victory. With the capture of Fort Detroit, most of the Michigan Territory was now in British hands. Many of the Native peoples who had so far stayed neutral in the conflict, now declared for the British. The militia and the Upper Canada legislature were also buoyed by Brock's success.

Canadians were exhilarated. They began to think there was a chance that the American invasion could be resisted after all. Brock had captured an entire army — more than double the size of his own — and taken control of a territory as large as Upper Canada. It was a tremendous feat. But of more immediate importance to Brock was the cache of weapons, supplies, and coin that the victory had brought the British forces.

He knew that the war had just begun. He also knew that if the Americans had any tactical sense at all, they would attack on several fronts. Reasoning that the enemy's next target would be the Niagara frontier, Brock handed over command of the Detroit area to one of his subordinates and hurried back across Lake Erie to Fort Niagara.

But before he reached the fort, he heard news that threatened everything he had achieved. Governor General George Prevost had negotiated a one-month truce with the Americans. The truce had gone into effect on August 8, a week before Brock had taken Fort Detroit, though no word had reached either the British or Americans there. Brock, eager to act on the momentum he had built, was bitterly disappointed. The Native peoples were outraged. They wondered if they had backed the wrong side.

In Niagara, Brock was hailed as a hero. He was a little stunned by the adulation he received but slowly began to "attach to it more importance than I was at first inclined." He used his new heroic status to convince the legislature to call up more militia, but he was unable to convince Prevost to build on these victories by launching an immediate attack on the American fortifications across the Niagara River.

In America, even while their General Hull was being court-martialled for cowardice, Brock had achieved a near mythic status as a man of unparalleled courage and honour. An incident that demonstrated this unfailing sense of honour occurred earlier in the war. A Canadian commander had landed his vessel along the Lake Erie shore and raided several American farms. When he heard about it, Brock was furious. He ordered the ship back under a flag of truce. The property that had not been destroyed was returned to the owners, along with funds to cover the rest.

A Thin Red Line

During the truce, Brock spread the 1000 regular troops and 600 militia along the 37-kilometre Niagara frontier, all the way from Fort George in the north to Fort Erie in the south. He concentrated most of them at Fort Erie and Chippawa, where everyone expected the Americans to attack first. He had a further 600 militia and Native warriors on standby.

Brock was under no illusions. He believed that the Americans were using the truce to reinforce their positions. And he was right. He arrived in Fort George on September 6, two days before the truce was scheduled to end. By this time, the Americans had managed to muster more than 8000 troops, half of them regulars. These troops were now gathered along the American side of the Niagara River.

Realizing he was facing a significantly larger force, Brock wrote to Prevost requesting reinforcements. Prevost refused. He still believed that no invasion would take place on either frontier as long as the British did nothing to antagonize the Americans. He instructed Brock to maintain a defensive posture only, and even asked him to consider abandoning Detroit and the Michigan area and move those troops east to the Niagara frontier. This was, of course, unacceptable to Brock. He knew the current support of the Canadian people, the militia, and the Native peoples was tied directly to his victory at Detroit. Abandoning that victory could very well lose him that support.

Brock was first and foremost a soldier. He obeyed commands. Even though he believed he could sweep the entire Niagara frontier if given the opportunity, he didn't attack. But nor did he abandon the Michigan territories.

The frustrated Brock knew the Americans would have to attack soon to keep their restless troops under control. A number of American regulars had already defected to the British, carrying with them tales of impatience and insurrection among the American regular troops and militia. The American militia was no happier with the war than the Canadians were. Most were reluctant to fight their former neighbours, and militia pay and rations offered them little incentive. Brock set up a system of beacon signals along the Niagara frontier to warn of the coming attack. Then he waited.

On the night of October 11, the few soldiers stationed at the village of Queenston, 10 kilometres south of Fort George, listened avidly to the sounds of a botched invasion attempt from the Americans. Armed, and anxious to start the fight, the Americans had boarded boats to take them across the Niagara River to the village. To their dismay, they discovered that all the oars had been stored aboard another boat. Unfortunately for them, that boat, and the sailor in charge of it, had disappeared. Whether by chance or design, no one was sure.

The Americans and Canadians sat out the night behind their own borders while a massive storm whipped up the already rough waters of the river. The wait took its toll on the soldiers of both sides. In the morning, Brock received word that his own soldiers in Queenston had threatened to shoot their superiors if action didn't begin soon. Brock immediately dispatched a trusted officer, Captain Thomas Evans, to investigate the mutiny and bring back some of the worst offenders. Evans did not have to ask what would happen to the mutineers he brought back. Years before, Brock had arrested a group of Fort George soldiers who had mutinied against their commander. The mutineers were taken out and shot in front of the entire company. While Brock could be humane, even jovial, he was also ruthless when necessary.

Brock also commanded Evans to negotiate an exchange of British soldiers and sailors with the American general, Stephan Van Renasselaer. When Evans returned that evening, he reported that he had released all the mutinying soldiers in Queenston, believing the group could earn their parole in the coming fight. The officer also told Brock that he had been denied entry into Van Renasselaer's camp. This incident, along with other news he had heard, made Evans conclude that an attack on Queenston was imminent.

Brock's staff officers dismissed Evans' report. After all, rumours of impending attack had been incessant since the ending of the truce more than a month before. Brock, although also skeptical, called up the Queenston militia and ordered them to join the two companies of the 49th Regiment, the Grenadiers Company and the Light Company, who were already there. The Grenadiers were in a stone guardhouse in the village. The Light Company was camped atop the escarpment above the village. With the militia and regulars, a mere 300 men guarded Queenston.

Brock the Brave
At 4 a.m. on October 13, 1812, Brock was awakened in his quarters in Fort George by the booming canons of a furious artillery assault on Queenston. Had the battle begun? Was Queenston the true target? Or was this a feint to draw attention away from the real attack on Fort George?

Anxious to see what was happening, Brock leapt onto his horse and galloped towards the battle, pausing only to order an artillery unit and a party of Mohawk warriors to follow him. His aide de camp, Macdonell, raced after his general, but he could not catch him. Two other aides, who had not even had time to dress, lagged hopelessly behind.

As Brock struggled through the mud on the ride to Queenston, he encountered a young York militiaman who had been dispatched to tell him the enemy had launched their attack. In the heat of battle, no one had thought of using Brock's carefully planned signal fires. Angry at the oversight, but excited at the prospect of battle, Brock urged his horse forward. The York Volunteers, a militia unit, were already moving towards the besieged village. Brock waved them on as he galloped past.

Queenston was a tidy little village with no more than 20 houses scattered within its boundaries. On that fateful morning, it had already survived Mother Nature's fury in the form of a wicked fall thunderstorm. It was now being buffeted by yet another tempest. This one was courtesy of the Americans — and far more deadly.

As Brock rode into the village, the Grenardiers cheered him. He saw they were holding the enemy — barely — and galloped past. He headed directly for the escarpment above the village, where the men of the Light Company were protecting the heights. As soon he reached the top, he ordered these men to go back down the hill to help the Grenardiers wrest control of the village.

Brock was left with only an eight-man gunner team. The men aimed the 18-pound cannon at the America shore, pounding the river and shoreline with artillery fire. Brock intently surveyed the scene below him. Cannons on both sides roared incessantly. Shells burst in the air above the river and the village. The bright, brief flare of muskets lit up the murky dawn. Across the water, he saw hundreds of the enemy waiting their turn to board the boats and cross to Queenston. Sailors valiantly rowed empty boats back to the American side to pick up more men, shells splashing into the water all around them.

Then Brock heard an unexpected and spine-chilling sound from behind him — a battle cry. He spun around to see an American force cresting the heights. The gunners barely had time to spike their gun, rendering it unusable, before they scattered down the hillside. Brock quickly followed, leading his horse by the reins, for he had not even had time to remount.

Once in the village, Brock took refuge in one of the abandoned houses. By this time, Macdonell had finally reached the village and found his general. Brock instructed him to send for reinforcements and then weighed his options. The situation was desperate. He could try to retake the heights without the help of the reinforcements, which would be extremely hazardous, or he could wait. Reinforcements would take too long to get there. The Americans would use that time to ferry over more men and consolidate their positions. Without control of the heights, Brock believed Upper Canada would be lost. Once the Americans gained a foothold in Queenston, they would have cut his thin red line along the Niagara frontier in two.

Brock was not a man to hesitate. With typical bravado, he mounted his horse and galloped through the village. He rallied some 200 soldiers, and an equal number of weary, dazed local militia — men he was now proud to lead. "Follow me boys," he yelled as he thundered toward the base of the ridge, where he took cover behind a wall. "Take a breath," he shouted a moment later, "you'll need it in a few moments."

The soldiers cheered.

Before the cheers had died away, Brock charged up the hill. His soldiers struggled to keep up on the slippery footing of wet leaves. No one was close enough to their general to urge him to slow down and take cover among them. Once again, Brock was an easy target. This time, he took a bullet in his wrist. The wound slowed him down, but he pressed on, waving his sword.

On the heights above them, the Americans had fanned out. Hidden among the trees and foliage, they continued firing their muskets at the British and

Canadian soldiers as they crested the hill. Many bullets found their mark. One found Brock. "Are you much hurt, Sir?" one of the militiamen asked anxiously. Brock did not reply. With his hand clutching his chest, he sank to the ground. The bullet had pierced his heart — he died instantly.

The stunned soldiers crowded around their fallen leader, barely able to grasp that Brock, a man who seemed invincible, was dead. Mud splattered his face, and blood soaked his jacket and the beaded sash. He no longer looked like the elegant general they knew; but he was not diminished in their eyes. As they stood rooted to the ground, a cannon ball sliced one of the men in two and the corpse fell on Brock's body. This prompted the horrified soldiers into action. They retreated, carrying their general's body back down the hill.

Even in death, Brock was victorious. His demise spurred on both the British and Canadian soldiers, who were now determined to avenge their fallen hero. Macdonell gallantly led two more unsuccessful attempts to retake the heights. He was wounded in the second attack and died later that night.

The reinforcements — soldiers and a group of very determined Mohawks — finally arrived and joined Brock's troops in the fight. Together, they pushed the Americans out of the village. On the ridge, the British, led by General Roger Sheafe, advanced on the American line with bayonets fixed. The line collapsed and the Americans fled to the edge of the escarpment. Some fell to their deaths; others managed to make it to the beach, where they waited in vain for boats that never came. Many others hid in the crevices of the escarpment, waiting for their leader to surrender.

He tried. He had sent two men on separate missions to surrender. Both had been killed by incensed Native warriors who had seen the Americans kill their men. Finally, the American commander went himself. He made it through, barely, and his surrender was accepted.

Brock's forces had won the day, recapturing both the heights and the village. But this was no bloodless victory. The American toll was 300 killed or wounded and 925 taken prisoner. The British and Canadians suffered only 15 deaths and 70 wounded. But the victory was bittersweet to soldiers and citizens alike because it had cost them their well-loved hero.

One young militiaman wrote to his brother, "Were it not for the death of General Brock and Macdonell, our victory would have been glorious... but in losing our man... is an irreparable loss."

A friend of Brock's from Quebec, one of the many ladies he had charmed, wrote, "The conquest of half the

United States would not repay us for his loss. By the faces of the people here you would judge that we have lost everything, so general is the regret everyone feels for this brave man, the victory is swallowed up in it."

On the morning of October 16, the caskets of Brock and Macdonell were carried from Government House in Newark to Fort George. Throngs of people came out to witness the solemn procession. Inside the fort, the pall-bearers carried the two caskets between rows of more than 5000 troops, militia, and Native warriors so they could pay their final respects.

A 21-gun salute broke the silence as Brock and Macdonell were lowered into a single grave. Moments later, the salute was echoed as soldiers on the American side also paid their respects to the fallen general.

Brock's confidence in Canada's ability to repel the Americans had been shared by very few others. With his death, Canadians had a hero to mourn and a common cause to rally behind. If they could not follow the general into battle, they would follow his vision.

For Tecumseh and the Native warriors, the loss of Brock was a terrible blow. They had lost the one British soldier they admired and trusted, the man who had promised them a homeland. But their lot had been cast. They would remain with the British to see the war to its end.

Issac Brock

Far away in England, church bells rang in Sir Isaac Brock's memory. For his capture of Fort Detroit, the Prince Regent had made him a Knight of the Order of Bath. But Brock had never learned of that honour.

In Brock's hometown on the small island of Guernsey, Channel Islands, his family crest was changed to include the figure of a Native warrior, reflecting his family's pride in the unique relationship Brock had forged with Tecumseh and the Native peoples of Canada.

In one short year, Brock had managed to inspire a nation. He was the stuff legends are made of. Following his death, the myth and legend of Brock became larger than the man himself. The soldier, who had wanted nothing more than to leave Canada, was destined to spend all of eternity there as a symbol of loyalty and courage. Brock left a legacy of confidence to the people of Canada; confidence in their leaders, and, more importantly, confidence in themselves. They were going to need both in the coming months.

Chapter 2
1813 – 1814
James Fitzgibbon

U ntil the autumn of 1812, the reality of war had not had much of an effect on the average citizen, so cross-border relations remained cordial. Canadian farmers in both Upper and Lower Canada continued selling their goods in American markets, and Vermont farmers supplied much of the beef consumed by British soldiers. Rationing was relatively new and, thus far, was not considered terribly onerous. More important, the battles had been confined primarily to military installations, and casualties had been light.

That all changed after October 13, 1812.

James Fitzgibbon

Dozens of Canadian militiamen had fallen along-side Brock at the bloody Battle of Queenston Heights. In the following months, the Canadians and British would win one battle only to lose the next. Territory was gained and lost so often, and so rapidly, that the border became blurred. Soldiers who had become separated from their units roamed the frontier not knowing which side of the border they were on.

The people of Upper Canada were now living in a perpetual battleground. Their farms were burned, their possessions looted, their men conscripted by the government, or imprisoned by the enemy. This cruel reality forced even the most apathetic civilians to choose sides. Some sided with the Americans, but the majority stood firm as Canadians. The bravery of some of these civilians helped turn the tide of the war in Canada's favour. Lieutenant James Fitzgibbon was fortunate enough to cross paths with two of these brave Canadians: Billy "The Scout" Green and Laura Secord.

James Fitzgibbon, The Soldier
Lieutenant James Fitzgibbon was a self-educated man. Unlike many of his fellow officers in the British army, he had earned his way through the ranks by recognition rather than through an exchange of coin. The son of a poor Irish farmer, Fitzgibbon joined the army at 17,

sailing with Lord Nelson against Napoleon. Shortly after his arrival in Canada in 1813 at the age of 33, he attracted the attention of Brock. Fitzgibbon had more than a hint of the brashness that was so much a part of Brock's character; the general recognized his potential and became his unofficial mentor. He helped the strong, ambitious Fitzgibbon to refine his manners and improve his diction, turning the soldier into a gentleman.

Fitzgibbon was a natural leader, and easily earned the respect and loyalty of his men. He was so well respected that he was able to persuade his commanding officer, Major General John Vincent, to allow him to form a special unit. Fitzgibbon handpicked the men from the 49th Regiment and trained them vigorously in guerrilla warfare. They had one purpose: to chase down, capture, or kill the renegade American soldiers who were terrorizing the population of the Niagara frontier.

The elite unit quickly established a fierce reputation on both sides of the border. The grey-green coveralls they wore earned them the nickname "The Green Tigers." But they called themselves "The Bloody Boys," a name that stuck. They roamed the Niagara region on horseback, frequently in disguise, hunting the most notorious of the American invaders. Canadians loved the Bloody Boys. Stories of their escapades encouraged some of the bolder young men to help them harass the invading Americans. Even those less brave did what they could to help Fitzgibbon and his men.

In April 1813, American warships sailed across Lake Ontario. The soldiers invaded and destroyed Fort York, then went on to loot the town of York (present day Toronto, Ontario.) A month later, they again turned their attention to the south and began another vigorous attack on the Niagara frontier. Their first foray was a successful attack on Fort George, where Fitzgibbon was stationed.

The young lieutenant, along with 1400 other men and their commander, John Vincent, were forced to abandon the fort. They marched inland towards Beaver Dams, where they were joined by other British troops escaping from both Fort Erie, at the southern end of the Niagara frontier, and Amherstberg on the western frontier. With retreat the only option, Vincent sent the militia back to their homes. It made little sense to continue to house and feed a volunteer army during a retreat, especially when many of them were needed at home on their farms.

The Americans chased the retreating British for four weeks. The militia, and indeed most of the population of the Niagara Peninsula, had every reason to believe that the British were abandoning them. In fact, Vincent had been ordered to abandon the peninsula.

His superiors considered it to be both indefensible and expendable. It was deemed important only because it served as a buffer between the Americans and Kingston, the capital of Upper Canada. Fortunately for the people of Niagara, Vincent was not willing to give up the area without a fight.

Once the troops were off the peninsula, Vincent halted his retreat and set up camp at Burlington Heights (near present day Hamilton, Ontario.) The British, now barely 1600 men strong, were about to face a force of nearly 3000 Americans. They needed an edge, and the daring James Fitzgibbon was just the man to provide it.

On the morning of June 5, Fitzgibbon dressed himself as a butter peddler. He made his way back along the peninsula to the American encampment near Stoney Creek, a village about 16 kilometres from the Canadian and British position. While selling his butter, he surreptitiously counted men and armaments. When he returned to his own camp he was able to report that the Americans were disorganized and their men and guns badly positioned. He had also found out the Americans were expecting reinforcements to arrive soon. He advised Vincent to attack immediately.

Billy Green, The Scout
At the same time Fitzgibbon had been reconnoitering in

the American camp, two young farmers — Billy Green and his brother Levi — were innocently roaming the woods on the Niagara Escarpment, high above him. The last thing they expected to see on their morning walk was the American army.

The Green family had moved to Canada from the United States 19 years earlier, just before Billy's birth. Until that day, Billy's sole claim to fame was that he was the first white child born in Stoney Creek. He was about to make another claim.

The brothers were not interested in the position or strength of the army; but they were not about to pass up the chance to have a little fun. Hidden in deep foliage, they watched as the American advance guard marched by on the way to attack the British in Burlington Heights. The boys began whooping like warriors, terrorizing the American soldiers. They laughed silently as the stragglers at the end of the column broke into a run to catch up to the rest of the troop. "I tell you those simple fellows did run," Billy recounted years later.

When the coast was clear, Billy and Levi made their way to the village, crossing the road the American troops had just marched along. They came across a lone American soldier who was winding a rag around his bootless foot. The American reached for his gun, but Levi was quicker. He grabbed a stick and struck the soldier. When the other soldiers heard their comrade's yells, they begin firing. Billy and Levi disappeared into the woods and ran back up the escarpment.

The brothers reached Levi's cabin safely. By then, a crowd of settlers, drawn by the sound of war whoops and gunfire, had come out onto the ridge to see what was happening. Billy and Levi joined them. They watched as the Americans traipsed through the village. Unable to resist a repeat performance, Billy whooped again and Levi answered him. One of the Americans fired at the hill, narrowly missing Levi's wife, Tina, and their infant daughter.

Billy and Levi hid in the woods while Tina retreated to the safety of a nearby trapper's hut. A group of soldiers knocked at the trapper's door and asked the terrified woman if she had seen any Natives. In a trembling voice, she told them a fierce band was roaming the mountain. The soldiers were convinced.

Once the Americans had gone, Billy went to Stoney Creek to check on his sister Keziah Corman and her husband Isaac. Keziah told him that Isaac had been arrested for answering insolently when the Americans asked for directions. Billy ran through the village and into the woods in search of his brother-in-law, whistling like a bird as he ran. Finally his whistles were answered by an owl hoot. It was Isaac.

Isaac had made his escape by pretending he was sympathetic to the American cause. He told the commander he was from Kentucky and was a first cousin to William Henry Harrison, the American Governor of Indian Lands. It was a truthful statement; his mother was Harrison's aunt. The commander promptly released Isaac and gave him the password so the soldiers would allow him through their lines.

Isaac had sworn not to give the password to the British — so he didn't. He gave it to Billy instead. Billy, now caught up in the excitement and committed to doing his part for Canada, borrowed a horse and started out for Burlington Heights to give the precious information to the British. He rode the horse until it was exhausted, then walked the rest of the way.

Billy arrived late that night, just as Vincent was preparing to attack. A night attack was an extraordinary action for an army that normally fought by traditional rules of war, but the situation called for drastic action. Darkness would be their ally; surprise their only hope.

Vincent had intelligence that the American cavalry would soon catch up with the infantry and they would then be in position to attack. The British had neither the arms nor the manpower to stage a frontal attack, and they could not withstand a frontal attack from the Americans. To make things worse, the British commanders believed

American warships would arrive any day.

Young Billy proved to be much more than a good luck charm to the British that night. Although they initially suspected him of being a spy, they eventually believed his story and took him to Vincent's commanding officer, Lieutenant Colonel John Harvey. Billy gave him the password and told him where and how the Americans were camped. Harvey asked Billy if he could lead them. When the lad gave him an enthusiastic yes, the officer gave him a corporal's sword and told him to take the lead.

Billy galloped off towards Stoney Creek. Occasionally he grew frustrated with the soldiers lagging behind him and went back to urge them to move more quickly. "It will be daylight soon," he cajoled. "That will be soon enough to be killed," one of the men replied laconically.

They reached the encampment just before dawn on June 6, 1813. Billy dispatched one sentry with his knife, but another guard managed to fire a shot, alerting his fellow soldiers. The British dashed forward, whooping like warriors while firing their muskets. The Americans met them, and the line of battle swung madly. In the blackness, British and Americans retreated and advanced, and enemies become indistinguishable from allies. On the left, the British line faltered until Fitzgibbon rode up and down restoring order. During the melee, two American generals were captured and the cannons were disabled. The American line broke and the troops scattered in retreat.

Major General Vincent, who had been eager to lead his troops against the Americans, did not witness this victory. He became separated from his men before the battle started and was soon lost. He wandered through the thick forest as the battle raged, sure that his forces had been defeated. Two soldiers found him the next morning — minus his hat and his dignity.

Some days later, when Harvey wrote his official account of the Battle of Stoney Creek, June 6, 1813, he made no mention of the hapless Vincent's misfortune, nor did he mention the brave adventurer Billy Green. In Stoney Creek, however, Billy became a folk hero, known throughout the region as "The Scout."

Cyrenius Chapin, The Raider
Upon their defeat at Stoney Creek, the Americans retreated to the safety of Fort George. After a hasty regrouping in their own camp, Vincent's troops followed the Americans. For three days they dogged the retreat. Luckily, they often came across wagonloads of supplies left behind by the fleeing Americans. Finally, the British and Canadians stood before the wooden palisades of the fort. They could not get in; the fort was too heavily

defended. But nor could the Americans break out in any significant numbers. They did, however, manage to make occasional raids on nearby farms and villages. One of the most infamous men in these raiding parties was Cyrenius Chapin, a doctor from Buffalo, New York. The doctor was well known for his ruthless plundering of the homes of local settlers. Fitzgibbon was disgusted by Chapin's rampages and was determined to put an end to them; the Irishman had come to love Canada and wanted to protect the civilians. He knew Chapin was in the fort. He was just waiting for a chance to capture him.

That chance came on June 19. Fitzgibbon heard that the doctor had slipped out of the fort with a raiding party, so he and his Bloody Boys began scouring the Niagara Peninsula looking for him. They had tracked the raiding party to the countryside around the village of Lundy's Lane (present day Niagara Falls, Ontario), almost halfway down the peninsula. Fitzgibbon, believing he would attract less attention on his own, told his men to wait outside the village.

On the road into the village, the wife of a local militiaman waved him down and told him that Chapin was just ahead with more than 200 men. She urged Fitzgibbon to flee to safety. But retreat was not something Fitzgibbon was prepared to do. His enemy was near; he was not about to let him go.

James Fitzgibbon

Fitzgibbon spotted a horse that belonged to one of the raiders. It was tied to a post outside a tavern. He went into the tavern and was immediately accosted by two raiders — one of them levelled a rifle at him. The brash Fitzgibbon extended a hand to the American and moved towards him in a friendly manner, as if he had recognized him as an acquaintance. This action confused the American for just long enough to allow Fitzgibbon to seize the rifle and order him to surrender. The other American took aim, but Fitzgibbon grabbed his rifle before he could fire.

During the ensuing struggle, the three men tumbled out of the tavern. The woman who had warned Fitzgibbon about the raiders was still on the road. She pleaded for help from several passing wagons, but the drivers did not want to get involved. Only a small boy answered her plea by throwing stones at the Americans. One of the raiders grabbed hold of Fitzgibbon's sword. This could have been the end of Fitzgibbon but for the innkeeper's plucky wife. The woman had rushed outside to watch the fight, still holding her baby. When she saw Fitzgibbon's plight, she put the baby down, ran forward, and kicked the sword from the American's hand. Within seconds she had scooped up her baby and disappeared into the tavern. Finally, the innkeeper arrived and helped Fitzgibbon disarm and arrest the Americans.

Chapin, who must have been somewhere nearby, escaped.

Laura Secord, The Heroine of Beaver Dams

A few days later, Vincent ordered Fitzgibbon to take up residence at the DeCew homestead near Beaver Dams. It was on the escarpment, about 30 kilometres southwest of Fort George. The house was to be the headquarters for Fitzgibbon and the Bloody Boys while they scouted the countryside looking for American troops who might have slipped out of Fort George.

Meanwhile, the Americans trapped inside the fort grew increasingly frustrated at not being able to break free and renew their campaign. They were also frustrated with Fitzgibbon and his Bloody Boys, who had been a nuisance for long enough. American spies had informed the incarcerated Americans that Fitzgibbon had been sent to the DeCew homestead to set up patrols. The commander at the fort sent out a message for more troops to come to their aid. The plan was that the troops would attack the hated Fitzgibbon first, and then go on to the fort and break through the line of soldiers and warriors holding siege. The rescuing troops, led by Lieutenant Colonel Charles Boerstler, were soon on their way.

A small advance party of Boerstler's men stopped

in Queenston to wait for the rest of the force. They chose a house at random and demanded the residents serve them dinner. They had chosen the home of Laura Ingersoll Secord.

Laura Secord and her husband James were both the children of United Empire Loyalists. Their families had fled to Canada during the American War of Independence almost 40 years before. James owned a shop, and the family was fairly prosperous. When war had been declared, James had joined the militia. At that time, the war had seemed distant. That was before October 1812 and the Battle of Queenston Heights, when the war had come to their doorstep — literally.

During that battle, Laura and her children sheltered at a farm outside the village. James stayed to fight. When she and the children returned, James was not there. She went to the battlefield to find him. The tiny woman struggled through the mud and bloodstained leaves, past the dead and wounded until, finally, she found him. He had been shot in the kneecap and shoulder and was in grave condition. Laura begged the help of a passing soldier and together they got James home. James lived, but his war service was over.

Even though no more battles were being fought in Queenston, American soldiers frequently looted the homes. Occasionally they burned them to the ground.

By the time Boerstler's men burst into the Secord home on June 21, 1813, it had already been raided twice.

The first time, Laura had protected the family heirloom, a rare collection of Spanish doubloons, by tossing them into a boiling cauldron of water hanging over the kitchen fire. The second time, according to some accounts, one of the American soldiers had boasted that once they had chased away the British, he would return to claim the Secord property as his own. Laura was infuriated by the arrogance of the American. She told him that the only land in Queenstown he would ever be able to claim as his own would be a six-foot grave. His companions returned later that day and told Laura that her prediction had proved true: the man had been killed in a skirmish with Canadian soldiers.

Now, with this third invasion of her home, the feisty 38-year-old was justifiably incensed. She reluctantly agreed to the soldiers' demand for dinner. With her husband still in bed recovering from his wounds, and no Canadian militia nearby, she had no choice. As the evening wore on, the Americans grew bolder, bragging that they were planning a surprise attack on Fitzgibbon at the DeCew homestead. They also talked about their grand plans to open up the entire peninsula to a massive American attack.

Laura had no details of how or when the attack

would take place. But she knew that Fitzgibbon was Canada's best chance for holding Niagara. She also knew that he had to be warned. Her husband was too severely injured to make the 30-kilometre journey to the DeCew home. She made up her mind to find another way to warn Fitzgibbon.

The next day dawned blistering hot. She rose early and put on a long cotton dress and white bonnet. Light slippers with low heels covered her feet. They would not offer much protection on her journey, but they would not raise any suspicion among the Americans. Laura did not want to be caught — the penalty for spying was death by firing squad. As dawn broke, she set out for her sister-in-law's home in the nearby village of St. David's, a small basket of preserves in hand.

Along the way, Laura was stopped twice by American patrols. She told them that she was going to visit her ailing brother in St. David's. This part of her story was true; Charles Ingersoll was indeed recuperating from a fever. The soldiers knew this, so they let her pass.

Laura was hoping that if her brother was too ill to go to Fitzgibbon, one of her older nephews would go instead. When she got to St. David's later that morning, she found that Charles was still feverish. Worse still, the boys had both joined the Canadian militia. She knew she had to make the 25-kilometre journey herself. According to some sources, Laura's niece accompanied her as far as Shipman's Corners (present day St. Catherines, Ontario), where the young woman collapsed from exhaustion.

Laura walked on the road as far as the village of Shipman's Corners, then travelled cross-country to avoid American patrols. She waded through a vast, treacherous quagmire known as Black Swamp, an area that teemed with rattlesnakes and was home to wolves and wildcats. She toiled across the swamp all afternoon, suffering terribly from the heat. Her courage almost failed her when she heard first one, then several wolf howls. By the time she reached the edge of the swamp, it was early evening. She was ragged, shoeless, and exhausted, but she still had a long way to go.

As Laura climbed up a steep escarpment, she realized she was being watched. Still, she forged ahead through the thick brush. At the edge of a clearing, she found herself surrounded by a group of Caughnawaga warriors. Once the shaken woman discovered they were loyal to the British, she tried to explain the situation to the chief and make him understand the urgency of her mission. The chief sent two warriors to escort the bedraggled Laura to Fitzgibbon. They arrived at the DeCew house just before midnight. Laura had been walking for almost 18 hours.

Laura told the amazed Fitzgibbon all she knew, and

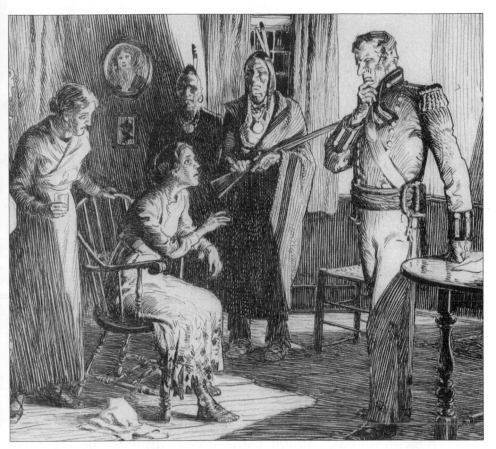

Laura Secord tells her story to Fitzgibbon

then collapsed. Fitzgibbon gently revived her and told his officers to escort her to the nearby farm of her friend, a Miss Tournay. There, Laura slept for 22 hours straight.

Fitzgibbon acted on Laura's information immediately. He sent the Caughnawaga warriors to watch for the American advance, and then made his own preparations to leave. The grateful lieutenant marvelled at the courage of this seemingly fragile woman. Years later he wrote, "I have ever since held myself personally indebted to her for her conduct upon that occasion."

During that long, terrible day, Laura's husband had been sick with worry. He had no idea if she had made it through the American lines or whether she had been captured. When she returned home, neither of them spoke openly of her journey. There were American sympathizers in the village. If these people found out she had warned Fitzgibbon, they would tell the Americans.

After the war, Laura broke her silence about her brave walk in order to get some compensation from the British. James had lost his shop and was unable to find work because of his war injuries. The family was destitute. Laura sent numerous petitions to the Prince Regent, and Fitzgibbon wrote a glowing letter in her support. Local politicians finally offered James Secord the position of magistrate, which he gratefully accepted. In 1860, when Laura was 83 years old, the Prince of Wales granted her a reward of £100.

James Fitzgibbon

The Battle of Beaver Dams

At midnight on June 22, 1813, Boerstler and the rest of his men reached Queenston. He put patrols in place to ensure that no citizen escaped to warn the British. He was, of course, unaware that this was now a useless precaution.

At daybreak on June 23, the Americans marched to St. David's. Eleven hours later, they ran into two Caughnawaga scouts. They shot one, but the other escaped and warned Francois Ducharme, their French Canadian commander. Ducharme, in turn, sent scouts to warn Fitzgibbon that the Americans had arrived.

Ducharme then led his several hundred warriors in an attack on the Americans, who were perched on the Niagara escarpment along a narrow strip of land lined on both sides by dense forest. The area was known as Beaver Dams. The Americans were just a few kilometres from their quarry, Fitzgibbon. But they did not have to go any farther to get to him. He came to them instead.

Ducharme's Caughnawagas, supported by several dozen Mohawks, fired from the forest. Boerstler's troops returned fire but soon used up their ammunition. The heavy fire from the forests showed no sign of letting up, and the exhausted soldiers knew they were vulnerable.

Meanwhile, Fitzgibbon had been concealed in the forest, waiting for his reinforcements to arrive before he joined the fight. Fitzgibbon had only 44 Bloody Boys with him. Although the reinforcements were nowhere in sight, he knew he had to act, so decided on an audacious bluff. With his customary aplomb, he walked out carrying a white flag and demanded that Boerstler surrender. He told the American that the British had his troops completely surrounded. He also added the now familiar falsehood that the Native warriors would massacre the Americans unless they surrendered immediately. Boerstler, not surprisingly, refused. He was not prepared to surrender to an army he had not even seen.

Carrying his bluff one stage further, Fitzgibbon suggested that the Americans send an officer to inspect the strength of the British troops. Then Fitzgibbon strode back into the forest on the pretext of asking his superior's permission to allow an American officer to see the troops. At this point, Fitzgibbon's bluff would have been exposed if it had not been for an incredible piece of luck. His hastily hatched plan was to get a British officer in full uniform to pose as his superior. But he did not have a single British officer in his party.

While he was desperately trying to come up with another plan, the advance party of his reinforcements came crashing through the forest. The relieved Fitzgibbon quickly ordered one of the British officers to play the role of the commanding officer. The officer, a man named John Hall, obediently accompanied Fitzgibbon back out into the clearing. When the American officer asked Hall to show his troops, the British soldier drew himself up and haughtily declared that it would be humiliating to display his force to the Americans. He assured the officer that it was large enough to annihilate Boerstler's forces.

Hearing this report, Boerstler asked for time to decide. Fitzgibbon gave him five minutes, and again used the lie that he would not be able to control the Native warriors for longer than that. Boerstler threw up his hands and begged to be saved from the warriors.

The outrageous bluff had worked. But now Fitzgibbon faced another hurdle. He had to figure out how to disarm 500 Americans with only his band of Bloody Boys, a handful of warriors, and a dozen Dragoons. Surrenders were usually very formal, with the surrendering army literally handing their weapons to the captors. Of course, Fitzgibbon could not allow this. If the Americans realized how small a group they had surrendered to, they would call off the surrender and continue the fight.

While Fitzgibbon was pondering his next move, his real commanding officer finally arrived with a small contingent of soldiers. As Fitzgibbon's superior, it was the commanding officer's prerogative to oversee the surrender. Unfortunately, he did not listen to Fitzgibbon's concern about the Americans seeing their meagre numbers. He told Boerstler to march his troops between the British troops, laying their weapons on the ground. Fitzgibbon, ever quick-witted, asked — in an unnaturally loud voice — if it was really a good idea to march the Americans past the still angry warriors. The Americans immediately tossed down their weapons.

When writing his report of the Battle of Beaver Dams, June 23, 1813, Fitzgibbon gave much of the credit to the Caughnawaga warriors. "With respect to the affair with Boerstler, not a shot was fired on our side by any but the Indians. They beat the American detachment into a state of terror; and the only share I claim is taking advantage of a favourable moment to offer them protection from the tomahawk and scalping knife."

The Caughnawaga suffered 15 deaths and 25 wounded that day. Unfortunately, the Mohawks took most of the spoils, leaving the Caughnawaga with next to nothing. John Norton, the Mohawk chief later observed, "... the Caughnawaga fought the battle, the Mohawks got the plunder and Fitzgibbon got the credit."

For the courage and ingenuity he had shown at the Battle of Beaver Dams, James Fitzgibbon was promoted to the rank of captain.

James Fitzgibbon

The War Drags On

A few weeks after the victory at Beaver Dams, Fitzgibbon and 40 Bloody Boys crossed the Niagara River to raid the American supply depot of Black Rock. Just as Fitzgibbon was about to launch the raid, a British force of about 200 regulars arrived. Their commander, Cecil Bishopp, had also planned to attack the supply depot, but he was worried he might not have enough men. When Fitzgibbon heard this, he threw his head back and laughed.

The two groups joined forces and successfully raided the depot. Fitzgibbon was ready to make a quick getaway, but Bishopp delayed their departure to load 40 barrels of much needed salt onto his boat. During that short time, American reinforcements arrived. In the ensuing fight, Bishopp and several of his soldiers were fatally wounded.

More than a year later, in August 1814, Fitzgibbon took part in the long, bloody siege of Fort Erie. In three months, the British had made three attempts to breech the walls of the fort. Each time, they had been driven back by the American gunners. The British succeeded on the fourth attempt, but reached only one of the fort's inner bastions. The British soldiers were discouraged and pessimistic about the outcome of the siege.

During this trying time, Fitzgibbon requested

permission to go to Kingston to get married. Permission was granted and he set off, promising to be back within three days. It seemed a strange request in the middle of a battle but, as always, Fitzgibbon had a purpose.

"There was a little girl I loved," he wrote to a friend, "and I knew that if I could but marry her before I was killed, and I a captain, she would have the pension of a captain's widow." He married his sweetheart on August 14, then left her on the church steps to return to a battle he did not expect to survive.

Fitzgibbon did survive the battle of Fort Erie. Many other British soldiers were not as lucky. The toll was 366 killed or wounded, and 539 taken prisoner or listed as missing. Against all odds, the gallant Irishman survived the entire war without serious injury. He returned to his wife, and they made their home in the country he had fought for and loved. When his wife died in 1846, Fitzgibbon retired to England, where he was made a knight of Windsor for his services to the Crown.

The old soldier longed to return to Canada, but he had duties that kept him in England. He wrote to a former comrade who still lived in Canada, "I sometimes exclaim 'Thank God, I have Canada to fall back upon.' Its future seems to me more full of promise than any other section of the human family. I long to be among you."

Chapter 3
1810 – 1813
Tecumseh

Brock fought in defence of the British Empire, and Fitzgibbon fought to protect the Canadian colony he had grown to love. Another of their allics, thc great chief Tecumseh, championed a third cause: that of the Native peoples.

No one, perhaps, felt the loss of Brock as keenly as did this renowned Shawnee Chief. The two shared a peculiar relationship. Both men were courageous, impetuous, and unwaveringly loyal to their cause. They were united by a shared goal — the defeat of the Americans — but neither man completely trusted the other. And if Brock was willing to use Tecumseh and the

Native warriors to win the war for the British, Tecumseh was equally willing to use the British to pursue his own vision. A vision of a United Native Empire.

A Man of Many Parts
Tecumseh was born in the Ohio Territories around 1768. His father had been killed in a battle with the settlers when Tecumseh was just six years old. His older brother, Cheesuaka, took responsibility for the young Tecumseh, training him to be both a warrior and a leader. He also trained him to distrust the settlers, although that particular training was hardly necessary. During his youth, Tecumseh watched the American government take more and more land from his people. This made him resentful. Then when Cheesuaka died a violent death at the hands of whites, he became dangerously bitter.

As an adult, Tecumseh warned his fellow peoples, "The white men aren't friends to the Indians…at first they only asked for land sufficient for a wigwam; now, nothing will satisfy them but the whole of our hunting grounds from the rising to the setting sun."

Tecumseh had participated in his first battle at the age of 15 and quickly earned a reputation as a courageous and ruthless warrior. But he was also compassionate. While still a young man, he watched a white prisoner being burned to death at the stake. He swore he would never again allow such atrocities in his presence.

When the war began, Tecumseh was 44 years old. He was, by most accounts, a well-built man with handsome features, copper skin, and clear hazel eyes. When wearing war paint and brandishing a tomahawk, he looked as fearsome as the most ferocious warrior. However, when delivering one of his eloquent speeches to the settlers, either in English or Shawnee, he appeared as dignified and composed as any British officer. No authentic likeness exists of Tecumseh because he refused to have his portrait painted. However, a wonderful description, written by one of Brock's aides, paints a picture of its own.

"Three small silver crowns, or coronets, were suspended from the lower cartilage of his aquiline nose; and a large silver medallion of George III ... was attached to a mixed coloured wampum string, and hung around his neck. His dress consisted of a plain, neat uniform, tanned deerskin jacket, with long trousers of the same material, the seams of both being covered with neatly cut fringe; and he had on his feet leather moccasins, much ornamented with work made from the dyed quills of the porcupine."

Not much is known about Tecumseh's personal life other than he eschewed liquor and, after being married four times, eventually chose to live without women in his life. Legend has it that between wives he fell in love with the 16-year-old daughter of a settler. It is said she taught him English and introduced him to the Bible and Shakespeare — his favourite play was *Hamlet*. The girl said she would marry him if he agreed to renounce his Indian ways and live as a white man. He refused. By the time war broke out between Canada and the United States in June 1812, he was a man with only one passion: his cause.

A Dream of Nation

His cause was clear and noble. He dreamed of an "Indian Nation" stretching from the Great Lakes to the Gulf of Mexico. He dreamed of uniting the First Nations in a confederation similar to that of the United States. If anyone was capable of achieving this, it was Tecumseh. The brilliant tactician and gifted orator managed to convince many of the Native leaders to support his vision. Many, but not all.

The British got their first glimpse of the charismatic Tecumseh in 1810, when they invited him to Fort Amherstberg to meet Matthew Elliott, the Indian Department representative. Elliott had been charged with the task of finding out whether the Shawnee and other groups would be loyal to the British if war broke out with the Americans.

Tecumseh

Elliott was a Loyalist who had come to Canada after the American War of Independence. He spent a lot of time with the Native peoples, and he respected them. He had expected Tecumseh to be lukewarm about the idea of supporting the British. He was surprised, and pleased, when Tecumseh declared his willingness to fight the Americans. Tecumseh made it clear that he had no interest in the quarrels between white people, but would willingly strike at the Americans if they continued to encroach on his land.

For several years, Tecumseh and his younger brother had been travelling among the different Native peoples in the United States and Upper and Lower Canada, encouraging the nations to join the cause. They were persuasive men. By 1811, more than 1000 warriors had left their homes to join the brothers in an inter-tribal settlement at the confluence of the Tippecanoe and Wabash Rivers (near present day Lafayette, Indiana.)

Tecumseh's brother was a mystic known as the Prophet. He was the group's spiritual leader, preaching that the encroachment of the settlers was a test from the Great Spirit. He maintained that the Native peoples must return to their old way of life or risk losing everything. He was feared by the whites but revered by his people. The settlement was dubbed Prophet's Town.

But for political and military leadership, the warriors, and the Prophet, turned to Tecumseh, who wanted to avoid bloodshed but was willing to use force if his words failed to stop the sale of land to the Americans. Tecumseh threatened to kill any chief who sold more land to the settlers.

Tippecanoe: A Catalyst to War
In the summer of 1811, several chiefs sold portions of their land to the Americans. The deals were brokered by the Governor of Indian Lands, William Harrison. The governor was well aware that Tecumseh and his brother would be furious and would likely harass the settlers on the recently purchased land. In an attempt to placate the brothers, Harrison invited them to a meeting at his estate near the town of Vincennes, Indiana.

Harrison, a shrewd man, thought out his strategy carefully. He summoned the chiefs who had sold the land and, as an added precaution, called up a large contingent of soldiers to guard him. Planning to intimidate Tecumseh, the governor arranged that he would be seated on a dais, and Tecumseh and his men would be seated below him. He had everything arranged to his satisfaction by the scheduled date of the meeting, and then he waited, and waited some more.

Tecumseh arrived on July 27 — three days late —

and not with the small escort he had been asked to bring, but with 300 heavily armed warriors. As Harrison would quickly learn, Tecumseh was not easily intimidated. He refused to sit below Harrison. Instead, he sat on the ground some distance away, forcing Harrison to come to him.

Tecumseh argued that the chiefs had no right to sell the land because it belonged to all Native peoples. "Sell a country!" he exclaimed. "Why not sell the air, the clouds, and the great sea, as well as the earth? Did not Great Spirit make them all for the use of his children?"

Tecumseh was so angry that the assembly feared he would loose his warriors on Harrison. But the warriors were held in check. They thundered away on their war ponies, leaving Harrison nervous, vexed, and impressed. In a report to his government, Harrison wrote: "If it were not for the vicinity of the United States, [Tecumseh] would, perhaps, be the founder of an empire that would rival in glory Mexico and Peru. No difficulties deter him. For years he has been in constant motion. You see him today on the Wabash and in a short time hear of him on the shores of Lake Erie or Michigan, or on the banks of the Mississippi, and wherever he goes he makes an impression favourable to his purposes. He is now upon the last round to put a finishing stroke to his work."

During the next two months, Harrison alternately fumed and worried as more Native people flocked to Tecumseh and his brother at Prophet's Town. Tecumseh continued travelling across the continent seeking to unite the scattered Native peoples. Finally, in the fall of 1811, Harrison made his move. While Tecumseh was in the southern states, Harrison had a fort built in the Indiana territory Tecumseh and the Prophet refused to yield. It was a show of force, but Harrison was also clearly trying to lure the impetuous Prophet into battle while his more cautious brother was not around to control him.

In late October, Harrison began marching his army towards Prophet's Town. On November 11, 1811, convinced the Americans were coming to destroy the settlement, the Prophet attacked the Americans. Harrison's troops fought them off easily. This show of American military strength made many of the Native warriors think twice about their allegiance to the brothers. Several hundred went back to their own lands, never to return to the cause. Others abandoned the settlement but regrouped somewhere safer. Within two days of the Battle of Tippecanoe, Prophet's Town was completely deserted. Harrison's soldiers rode in and razed it to the ground.

When Tecumseh returned from his journey to find Prophet's Town in ruins and his followers scattered, he swore vengeance on Harrison and all his kind. The Americans sent envoy after envoy to Tecumseh in an effort to win him over, but the die had been cast. Tecumseh had decided to throw in his lot with the British. He sent runners to inform all the First Nations of his decision. Twelve responded, each sending two political chiefs and two war chiefs. By May of 1812, Tecumseh had recruited another 600 men. They waited patiently for the war to begin.

The Battle is Joined
By the time war was declared, Tecumseh had already been tracking American movements and reporting them to the British. One of his quarries was Brigadier General William Hull, the unlucky soldier whose mail had been intercepted when the British captured the *Cuyahoga Packet* on June 21,1812.

In July, Hull had crossed into Upper Canada from Fort Detroit and taken the village of Sandwich on Canada's western frontier. His next target was the nearby Fort Amherstberg. He was not sure if he had enough men to take the fort, so he decided to send out bands of militia to test the strength of the British. Tecumseh and his warriors were watching.

When the militia were halfway between Sandwich and Fort Amherstberg, Tecumseh's warriors swooped down on them. The men were terrified. Against the orders of their officers, they retreated. When the officers threatened to shoot the deserters, they told them they would rather be shot by one of their own than killed by the warriors.

Tecumseh, along with British and Canadian troops, upset Hull's plans further. On August 5, 1812, they crossed the border into Brownstown, Michigan, and attacked a wagon train carrying provisions for Hull's army. This disaster, combined with the news that Brock's troops had captured Fort Michilimackinac, prompted Hull to withdraw his troops from Canadian soil and return to Fort Detroit. But even there he was not safe from Tecumseh.

The warriors remained lurking in the dense woods between Brownstown and Fort Detroit, waiting for another wagon train of supplies. As the soldiers guarding the convoy passed Brownstone, they saw the impaled corpses of their fallen comrades from the battle the week before. Tecumseh had left them there in an effort to intimidate the Americans. It worked. In the battle that followed, the Americans were once again routed.

After that battle, Tecumseh returned to Fort Amherstberg, where he had his first meeting with General Brock. Tecumseh aligned himself with Brock, a man he would be proud to follow into battle. Within a

Brock and Tecumseh meet for the first time

few days, Tecumseh and his warriors played a strategic role in the bloodless capture of Hull's troops and Fort Detroit.

Hull, who lived out his days in disgrace, blamed Tecumseh and his warriors for his defeat. Brock, surprisingly, failed to mention Tecumseh in his official correspondence about the fall of Detroit. And yet in a later correspondence, he admitted that losing the allegiance of Tecumseh could prove fatal to the war. In that same correspondence, Brock reminded the British political leaders of their promise to support a Native confederation south of the Great Lakes. Tecumseh saw that Brock was keeping his word, and that was all that mattered to him.

A Man of Principle

Tecumseh was also a man of his word. He demonstrated this at the surrender of Fort Detroit by keeping his promise to prevent a massacre. He was also compassionate. Stories of his acts of kindness soon circulated and were retold in barracks and cabins on both sides of the border.

One story involved a man of the cloth — an American minister captured at the surrender of Fort Detroit. Brock's deputy, Lieutenant Colonel Henry Proctor, had been put in charge of the surrender. He was an officious man and was going to imprison the minister because he would not swear allegiance to the Crown. Tecumseh felt this was wrong and protested. Proctor ignored Tecumseh. Angry over this injustice, the chief threatened to break his alliance with the British. Proctor reluctantly released the minister.

Another story involved a young American boy. Tecumseh saw the boy tending two oxen. His men needed food, so he took the oxen but promised to compensate the family. However, when Tecumseh asked the Indian Department representative to pay for the oxen, Elliott declared the animals were spoils of war and refused to pay. Tecumseh insisted, and also demanded an extra dollar to pay for the boy's time and trouble in collecting payment.

The End of a Dream
At the beginning of August 1812, Tecumseh felt confident his dream of a Native confederacy would soon be a reality. He was allied with the winning side and he had finally convinced Walk-in-Water, a Wyandot chief, to cross to the British side. This was of critical importance to Tecumseh's vision. The Wyandot were a senior nation. Where they went, others would surely follow.

Then he heard that the British Governor General had negotiated a ceasefire. Tecumseh was furious. His dream would never come true unless he could fight, and conquer, the Americans. Like Brock, Tecumseh knew that the British and Native peoples had to strike before the Americans had an opportunity to move more men and troops to the Niagara front or the western front.

Disgusted with his allies, Tecumseh left the battlefront and again went to the southern states to convince the Native peoples there to join his confederacy. The British didn't see him again all that winter. However, Tecumseh realized his fortunes were now irrevocably tied to the British. Therefore, he and his 2000 men rejoined them at Amherstberg in the spring of 1813. There, he learned that Brock had been killed at Queenston Heights. It was a devastating blow. Tecumseh was sorry to lose a man he respected. But he was even more concerned about what Brock's death would mean for his dream of a Native confederacy. To add to his misery, he knew he would now have to give his allegiance to Brock's successor, Lieutenant Colonel Henry Proctor — a man he had little use for. Proctor was not the commander his predecessor had been.

Men of Lesser Valour
On January 19, 1813 — while Tecumseh was in the south — Proctor crossed the frozen Detroit River to launch a counterattack against the Americans who had taken the

Canadian settlement of River Raisin (present day Monroe, Michigan). He was accompanied by Native warriors under the leadership of Roundhead, a Wyandot chief. The battle was short and savage. The British took 500 American prisoners. But the nervous Proctor almost immediately retreated to the relative safety of the village of Brownstown and left the American prisoners in the hands of Roundhead and his warriors.

There was no Tecumseh to maintain order. Rounhead's warriors murdered many of the prisoners and held the others for ransom. Thereafter, "Remember the River Raisin!" would become a rallying cry for the American militia.

The Lull before the Storm

In October 1812, Governor Harrison, who was by then a Brigadier General, took command of the American Army of the Northwest. During the winter of 1812 – 1813, he ordered a fort to be built at Meigs across the lake from Fort Amherstberg. It was one of the strongest forts of its time.

In early May 1813, Tecumseh and Proctor were sent to Fort Meigs with a combined force of 3000 men. Attempts to breach the walls using heavy artillery proved futile. Tecumseh and his men were restless, but they stayed and held siege.

A few days later, on May 5, American reinforcements arrived by boat. As they moved from the banks of the River Maumee to the fort, Tecumseh sent a handful of warriors to harass their flanks. With the massacre of River Raisin still fresh in the Americans' minds, half the reinforcements chased the warriors, following them deep into the forest.

It was a trap. Tecumseh was waiting there with the rest of his men. By the time the fight was over, 650 Americans had been killed or captured. The warriors marched the prisoners to the British Fort Miami (present day Fort Wayne, Indiana). First the captured Americans were stripped of their clothes and possessions, then the harassment turned deadly, and several prisoners were murdered. It was beginning to look like a re-enactment of the River Raisin. But this time, Tecumseh was near. As soon as he found out what was happening, he berated his warriors and demanded they stop. The terrified prisoners were then left alone.

Meanwhile, Proctor and his men had been continuing the siege of Fort Meigs. When Tecumseh returned from Fort Miami, he pressed Proctor to make a second attack, but not directly on the fort. The warrior proposed an ingenious plan. He knew the Americans had sent for more reinforcements, so he suggested the British and Native warriors trick the Americans into believing these reinforcements had arrived, and that they were being attacked. The warriors and the British soldiers moved out of sight of the fort, where they yelled, screamed, and fired their muskets. Tecumseh expected the Americans to leave the fort to come to the aid of their reinforcements, and when they did, they would get a nasty surprise. The ploy almost worked. The men in the fort heard the sounds of a pitched battle and were anxious to engage, but their commander held them back. He suspected a trick.

Again, Tecumseh was frustrated and wanted to leave. Proctor, realizing he could not keep Tecumseh there any longer, withdrew his troops. During the next few weeks, Proctor and Tecumseh suffered a string of humiliating defeats. Dozens of Tecumseh's men deserted. A British victory — and Tecumseh's dreams — seemed to be slipping away.

On September 10, 1813, British and American battleships waged a battle on Lake Erie. Proctor and Tecumseh watched from Fort Amherstberg while the British suffered their first naval defeat. Proctor, terrified of losing the Native alliance, tried to convince Tecumseh that the British had won the battle.

Tecumseh, of course, was no fool. He knew the British had been defeated, and he suspected they were planning to retreat. Retreating from his old enemy

Harrison was unthinkable to the proud chief. He had no faith in Proctor, so he turned to Matthew Elliot, the Indian Department representative. Tecumseh told Elliot he and his warriors would turn on the British and cut them to pieces if Proctor retreated. His threat was taken seriously; Tecumseh's warriors outnumbered the British regulars three to one.

On September 18, Elliot brokered a meeting between Tecumseh, Proctor, and the military advisors. Tecumseh accused the British of breaking their promise and abandoning his people. He reminded the assembly that they had not yet seen an American soldier in Amherstberg, and that they had yet to be defeated on Canadian soil. Proctor then made his case for retreat. The British would, he promised, meet the enemy at a more strategic location along the Thames valley, just 60 kilometres to the northeast. This would draw the Americans toward the east, deeper into Canadian territory and farther from reinforcements and supplies.

Tecumseh called Proctor a "miserable old squaw,' and accused the British of being "a fat animal that acts proud but drops its tail between its legs when challenged." But his words did not persuade. The decision to retreat had been made. Tecumseh was trapped in his alliance with Proctor; he had no choice but to follow the retreat. With great misgivings, he told his warriors, "We are going to follow the British, but I fear I will never return."

Proctor led the retreat. Within a few days, the British had abandoned all of the Michigan territory captured by Brock the previous year. Appalled by the lack of definitive action, and believing the British to be facing a defeat, half of Tecumseh's warriors deserted during the retreat.

The Storm

Finally, Proctor halted the retreat at a Native village called Moraviantown (near the present day town of Chatham). Tecumseh and the warriors scouted behind the troops and acted as a rear guard. In an effort to delay the advance of the Americans, Tecumseh stopped a few kilometres south of the village to destroy a bridge and skirmish with American scouts. But this did not slow Harrison's troops for long.

That evening, Tecumseh stopped at a mill while he waited for some of his warriors to catch up to him. The settler who owned the mill, Christopher Arnold, was terrified. A band of Native warriors had burned his neighbour's mill a few days before, and he thought he was in for the same treatment. Tecumseh knew that his warriors had been told to burn everything that might be of use to the Americans. But he realized the settlers were low on food and depended on the mill. He stayed the night to protect the mill from his own men.

The next morning, October 5, 1813, Tecumseh asked Arnold to watch for American scouts while he waited in the woods, ready to gallop off to warn the British at the first sign of them. He told the miller to pretend he was digging and to throw up a shovel of earth as soon as he saw the scouts. Arnold readily agreed. However, Tecumseh's sharp eyes found the scouts first and he was gone before Arnold had a chance to give him the signal. On his way to join Proctor, Tecumseh performed another act of charity. Arnold had told him that his brother-in-law's family had no food. The miller had wanted to take them some flour, but was afraid to venture out. So, on his way to join the troops, Tecumseh rode by the brother-in-law's house and tossed a bag of flour at the front door.

Tecumseh reached the troops and began to prepare for combat. He was still eager to fight, but had great misgivings about the looming battle. Proctor had not discussed strategy with him, the troops had not eaten in days, they were low on ammunition, and they were greatly outnumbered. Proctor had barely 500 regulars and militiamen. Tecumseh now commanded only 500 warriors. Harrison was fast approaching with more than 3000 well-armed men.

Tecumseh directed the battle strategy. He positioned his warriors on the far edge of a great swamp, and placed Proctor and his men to the left on some high ground between the Thames River and the swamp. He told the militia to take up a position between the two groups.

Reviewing the position of the British, Tecumseh cautioned Proctor to stand firm. Then he returned to the swamp to wait. There was now no trace of the compassionate, literate man. With war paint on his face, and hate in his eyes, he was the quintessential warrior.

The American troops arrived at the battleground. The two armies faced each other for several hours, barely 275 meters apart, while the Americans formed their lines. Finally, they were ready for combat. One battalion charged the British, then a group of Kentucky militiamen advanced towards Tecumseh. The hardened men yelled, "Remember River Raisin," as they spurred their horses forward. As Tecumseh had predicted, the horses got bogged down in the thick marsh, and the Americans were forced to continue on foot. Tecumseh's warriors cut them down.

This respite did not last long. The British line had broken and Proctor's soldiers were running for their lives. Tecumseh and his men had been abandoned. Harrison's troops closed in on the warriors. When the warriors ran out of ammunition, they fought on with their tomahawks. Tecumseh's chilling war cry echoed through the forest; then it was silenced.

Words Tecumseh had spoken just a few days earlier might still have been on his mind as he fell. "Our lives are in the hands of the Great Spirit. We are determined to defend our lands, and if it is His will, we wish to leave our bones upon them."

The great chief was never found. It is generally believed the warriors took his body with them when they retreated. There is no official record of Tecumseh's death, and no official marker over his final resting place. But, to this day, the Shawnee elders say they know where he is buried and that the location of his grave has been passed down from one generation of select leaders to the next.

Wherever Tecumseh lies, the hopes of a Native peoples' confederacy are buried with him. The grand alliance between the Native peoples and the British was finished. The last of the nations made peace with the Americans, and the lands that Tecumseh had fought to keep free were sold to settlers. The Native peoples of Tecumseh's generation lived the rest of their lives on small parcels of reserved lands.

"The great barrier was broken," wrote one of his followers. "It was my last fight. My heart was big then,

Tecumseh filled it. It has been empty ever since."

After the Battle of the Thames, Proctor was court-martialled for negligence and incompetence. Suspended from his post, he lived out the rest of his days in disgrace. Brigadier General Harrison, lacking adequate supplies for the coming winter, was unable to capitalize on his victory. He retreated back to Fort Detroit.

The war was at a stalemate once more, and the borders were much the same as they had been in the early months of the war.

Chapter 4

1812 – 1814
Charles-Michel
de Salaberry

In the spring of 1813, with their advance into Upper Canada at a standstill, the Americans turned their attention to the less heavily defended Lower Canada. Their aim was to capture Montreal and cut off the critical British supply line from the Atlantic. They discussed their plans in detail, unaware that Canadian spies were eavesdropping and taking the information back to a young lieutenant colonel in the British army. This officer, a French Canadian aristocrat with the imposing name of

Charles-Michel de Salaberry

Charles-Michel d'Irumberry de Salaberry, was aware of every move the Americans made.

De Salaberry was a career soldier both by choice and by tradition. For centuries, his forebearers had served in armies under the kings of France. When one of his ancestors moved the family to Upper Canada (then called New France) in the 1700s, the de Salaberrys continued the military tradition. After the British defeated the French in Lower Canada in 1759, part of the family returned to France. Those who stayed gave their allegiance to the French in Canada, rather than to some distant king in France. Charles' father served in various political positions with the British administration, so it was natural the family would support the British against the Americans in the war of 1812.

Charles de Salaberry was born in Beauport, Lower Canada, in 1778. He joined the British army at age 14, serving in the West Indies and then in Holland, fighting Napoleon. His mentor and sponsor in the military was none other than the Duke of Kent, the father of the future Queen Victoria. The Duke spent several years in Lower Canada, where he became great friends with Charles' father.

Despite his promising military career in England, de Salaberry wanted to return to Canada and his family. He was finally transferred home in the spring of 1812,

Charles de Salaberry

just before the war began.

De Salaberry was 34 when he returned from England, a seasoned soldier and a man to be reckoned with. He was average height, but incredibly strong and well proportioned. For all his physical attributes, it was his personality that made him stand out from his fellow soldiers. One of de Salaberry's superiors referred to him as "my dear Marquis of cannon powder," making reference to both his aristocratic ancestry and his bold, intimidating manner. As was to be expected of a man of his background, honour meant more than life to de Salaberry — a scar on his forehead bore witness to that. While he was in Europe, a Prussian officer had bragged about killing a French Canadian. De Salaberry had told the Prussian to follow him outside so he could try to kill another. After the duel, only de Salaberry had walked away.

The French Canadians were the wild card in the British deck of support. No one was really certain where their loyalty would lie in the coming conflict. The Americans were counting on the French Canadians to support them. They felt the French Canadians were repressed under the British and would be anxious to escape from British "tyranny." But they were wrong. Most French Canadians disliked and distrusted American-style democracy. They were eager to protect their religion, culture, and language; the British promised these would be protected under their administration. However, even though the French Canadians sided with the British, they resented being forcibly conscripted.

The War of 1812 Against the States

In July 1812, the British sent Governor General George Prevost to Montreal to announce the forced conscription of 2000 bachelors into the militia. The French Canadians rose up in protest, and there was a full-fledged riot in the village of Lachine. The British rushed in. By the time they restored order, hundreds of men had been arrested and two civilians had been killed. A far better diplomat than he was a soldier, Prevost pardoned all but the ringleaders of the riot and promised to preserve French Canadian cultural rights within the militia.

The Voltigeurs

Immediately after the riots, Prevost also had the foresight to ask the dashing and popular de Salaberry to recruit and train a French Canadian militia unit they would call the Voltigeurs (the literal translation of this word is "equestrian" but de Salaberry's Voltigeurs were a light infantry, not a cavalry unit).

De Salaberry drew his men from the hardiest of French Canadian stock — they were all former fur traders, trappers, and adventurers. Dressed in their distinctive grey uniforms and fur hats, the Voltigeurs were an efficient, deadly fighting force, as comfortable in the woods as they were on the battlefield. De Salaberry drilled them relentlessly until they evolved into one of

Charles-Michel de Salaberry

Canada's best fighting units.

When Prevost first presented the idea to de Salaberry, he promised him the rank of lieutenant colonel, a far more prestigious rank than he already held. The condition was that he had to recruit 380 men. De Salaberry's recruitment drive was wildly successful. Each recruit was offered immediate pay, along with the promise of 20 hectares of land at the completion of his service. De Salaberry upped the ante by telling his captains that they would receive no pay until they had recruited their own complement of militiamen. That was not a problem.

The ranks filled quickly and de Salaberry soon had his 380 men. The wily Prevost promptly raised the minimum number of recruits to 500 men. De Salaberry was justifiably angry at the trick. However, he was a dedicated military man so accepted the new orders. By September 1812, he had met the new quota and was given the promised reward.

De Salaberry had recruited most of the officers from among his friends and members of his large extended family. This initially posed a problem, but the officers quickly learned that the affable man who attended their balls and family parties was a very serious soldier. He would brook no disrespect and he was very firmly the man in charge.

Despite, or perhaps because, he was such a harsh taskmaster, he quickly earned the respect of his men. The same men who earlier in their training had complained that he was impossible to please would later be his most loyal admirers. It did not hurt that his rigid training had made them into a confident fighting force, both individually and as a unit. Their growing esprit des corps was tied directly to their commander, as this Voltigeur battle songs shows:

There's our Colonel
With Satan in his soul
Who'll be the death of us all
There was no beast of prey
That would dare stand in his way
You'll find our Colonel is unique.

The Voltigeurs had decided that if de Salaberry could intimidate them, he could not help but strike terror into the hearts of their enemies. Confidence was a powerful motivator and de Salaberry was nothing if not a confident commander. Perhaps he was a little too confident.

In late November 1812, two of de Salaberry's spies, David and Jacob Manning, informed him that a large force of American troops was advancing towards the Canadian border, intending to attack Montreal. De Salaberry was so certain that the 500 Voltigeurs and

Native warriors he commanded could hold off the 3000 Americans, that he did not bother to inform his superiors that the Americans were on the way — an action that could have earned him a court martial. It was a telling action. De Salaberry's arrogance put him in frequent conflict with his superiors, particularly Prevost, but it was this very arrogance that made him such a deadly threat to the Americans.

De Salaberry led his men to La Colle, a small village on the Canadian side of the Richelieu River, just north of Lake Champlain. About 45 kilometres south of Montreal, and a mere 20 kilometres north of the American encampment at Plattsburgh, New York, the community guarded the Richelieu River and access to the St. Lawrence and Montreal. De Salaberry knew that La Colle was the most likely entry point for the American force. Sure enough, in the early hours of November 27, 1812, an advance guard of about 800 American soldiers crossed La Colle Creek. De Salaberry and his men were waiting for them in a mill, a fortified stone building.

The Voltigeurs, along with their Mohawk allies, held off the Americans for as long as they could but finally, badly outnumbered, they retreated into the surrounding forest. It was not yet dawn. The Americans, now in possession of the mill, prepared to pursue the Voltigeurs. But before they could regroup, they were attacked again. The Americans fought furiously, but when dawn broke, they threw down their weapons in dismay. In the darkness and confusion, they had been fighting another unit of their own militia — a unit that had crossed the creek just hours after they had.

Making use of this unexpected advantage, de Salaberry launched a counterattack. The Americans, devastated and demoralized by the recent battle with their own comrades, were too shaken to fight. They hastily retreated back across the border. It was 12 months before they attempted another invasion of Lower Canada.

While the Americans were licking their wounds, de Salaberry stepped up his recruiting efforts and continued to drill his men. By the summer of 1813, he had recruited enough Voltigeurs to spare four companies — about 500 men — to help reinforce the troops currently fighting the Americans on the Niagara Peninsula. De Salaberry and his men also helped protect a British flotilla on Lake Champlain that summer, providing cover while the flotilla harassed the Americans.

In the fall of 1813, the Americans were again preparing to take Montreal. Prevost knew the enemy was shifting its focus from Niagara to Lower Canada, so he ordered reinforcements. However, they would still be greatly outnumbered. Once more, the British and

Charles-Michel de Salaberry

Canadians had to fool the Americans into believing they had huge armies. De Salaberry did this by marching his Voltigeurs from town to town and back again, much to the displeasure of the men.

The Battle of Chateauguay
In late September, the Americans began moving their troops into Lower Canada. This time, they had a sophisticated strategy: a two-pronged attack on Montreal. The plan was for one army to march along the banks of the Chateauguay River, while a second, larger force made its way up the St. Lawrence River by boat. The two rivers run parallel to each other, the Chateauguay running slightly to the south and joining the St. Lawrence a few kilometres south of Montreal. The two armies would meet near Kahnawake, about 30 kilometres south of Montreal, to converge on the city. The invasion force was huge — there were more than 10,000 soldiers.

The first army was led by General Wade Hampton. Its primary purpose was to divert attention from the main force that was currently massing at Sacket's Harbor, New York, and preparing to sail up the St. Lawrence. As Hampton's troops headed towards the Canadian border, the spy David Manning counted the guns, wagons, and soldiers. But Manning had more than mere numbers to report to de Salaberry. To everyone's surprise, 1400 New York Militiamen had refused to cross the border into Canada. By U.S. law, militiamen could not be forced to fight on foreign soil. The units from the northern states did not want to fight people they considered neighbours and friends. Nor were they anxious to be out in the elements during winter.

Many of the militia who decided to stay with their general were from the southern states. They were poorly clothed and completely unprepared to face a harsh Canadian winter. Manning also learned about the other American force that was heading up the St. Lawrence under the command of Major General James Wilkinson. De Salaberry was well pleased to have learned so much.

Hampton, although furious about the loss of so many of his militia, still felt confident about the coming attack. After all, he had more than 4000 men with him. On September 21, he created a diversion at the town of Odelltown, just inside the Canadian border. The Americans surprised the small group of British soldiers stationed there, killing three and capturing six.

De Salaberry knew the Americans had crossed into Canada, but the force he commanded was far too small to launch any kind of counter offensive. The best he could do was keep the Americans contained inside Odelltown. To that end, he sent out small units of Mohawks to intercept the American patrols. One of these units took down an American patrol. Fear of further encounters with the Native warriors kept the Americans inside the town. Thus, they remained ignorant of how very small de Salaberry's force really was. Faced with what they believed would be a long, tough fight, and hampered by a shortage of water, Hampton once again retreated back across his own border.

As soon as de Salaberry's scouts reported that Hampton's forces had abandoned Odelltown, de Salaberry led his men on a forced 24-hour march to the Chateauguay Valley. He knew Hampton would return and would then take his troops along this valley. The Canadian wanted to be there to greet him. De Salaberry left detachments of soldiers along the way to serve as communication outposts. He finally reached the valley, where he set up camp and waited for Hampton.

Meanwhile, Hampton had set up camp at Four Corners, a small town just inside the American border at the southern end of the Chateauguay Valley. This was about 15 kilometres from de Salaberry's camp. When de Salaberry learned of the Americans' whereabouts from his spies, he sent a few units of warriors and Voltigeurs to pepper the encampment with sniper fire. They terrorized the camp every night for two weeks. The Americans were so alarmed that they would not venture outside the encampment at night.

On October 1, de Salaberry received orders from Prevost to raid the encampment. It seemed like a suicide mission — de Salaberry's several hundred Voltigeurs and warriors against Hampton's several thousand militiamen. De Salaberry later wrote to his father that he suspected Prevost was trying to get rid of him. In spite of this, de Salaberry followed orders and stormed the camp.

The Americans quickly recovered from their surprise and launched a massive counterattack. During this attack, the Mohawks withdrew twice. Both times, de Salaberry brought them back. But on the third withdrawal, they were gone for good, taking a number of Voltigeurs with them. Only de Salaberry and four of his men were left to fend off the Americans. When night fell, the five exhausted men were able to slip away. Further attacks were out of the question.

De Salabery returned to his camp. He knew that Hampton's plans had not changed and that he and his men would soon be marching along the banks of the Chateauguay River to join up with the other invading force at Kahnawake. He took his men along the same route and ordered them to destroy bridges and strew felled trees across the path behind them.

The young lieutenant colonel was determined not to allow Hampton to reach Kahnawake, so he searched for a suitable area to make a stand against the huge force. Finally, at a series of sharp ravines where the English River flows into the Chateauguay, de Salaberry found his battlefield. The thick bush, blocked roads, and burned bridges had slowed Hampton's troops, giving de Salaberry the precious time he needed to prepare. His men fortified the ravines with "abatis," felled trees that were piled atop one another with their tops pointing downwards.

In the meantime, Prevost, who was in Kingston, had finally realized that Montreal was the Americans' main target. He made plans to take reinforcements to de Salaberry by land. But first he sent for Lieutenant Colonel "Red George" Macdonell — so named for his flaming red hair — and asked him to take a battalion to de Salaberry by boat. When Prevost asked Red George when he and his men could leave, the unruffled lieutenant replied, "Right after we finish supper." The soldiers hastily rounded up some boats and set off from Kingston on the treacherous St. Lawrence. They were caught in a blinding storm but forged on. They reached de Salaberry 60 hours later, an incredibly short time for having to travel a distance of more than 200 kilometres in such difficult conditions.

Red George reached de Salaberry on October 24. De Salaberry was happy to see the reinforcements, but he knew the extra numbers would not ensure victory. They were outnumbered three to one. It was time to try another bluff.

By this time, Hampton's troops were very close. Close enough to see what they thought were hundreds of reinforcements marching towards de Salaberry's camp. De Salaberry had used Brock's ploy of having the same men march back and forth wearing what looked like different uniforms each time. Not actually having any different uniforms, the men just turned their jackets inside out so the white lining showed.

Hampton was fooled into believing de Salaberry's force was twice the size of his own. Therefore, he dismissed the idea of a head-on assault. Instead, on October 25, 1813, he sent a force of 1500 men into the forests to attack de Salaberry's flanks. The Voltigeur scouts detected them. Red George and his men, along with a group of Voltigeurs, engaged the Americans and fought them off.

That afternoon, Hampton decided he would have to try a head-on assault after all. The American troops advanced toward the ravines. De Salaberry fired the first shot. There was a furious exchange of fire and de Salaberry ordered his men to take cover behind the abatis. Thinking that the Canadians and British were retreating, the Americans began to cheer.

De Salaberry encouraged his men to return the victory shouts. These shouts came from the top of every ravine. Then Red George's men picked up the shouts from their reserve position in the woods. The Mohawks added to the ruckus with their war whoops. The Americans had stopped cheering. They fired volley after volley into the woods at what they believed to be thousands of warriors. Finally, de Salaberry sent his buglers into the woods to sound an imaginary advance.

Silence fell over both armies. De Salaberry called out to one of his Voltigeurs in French, warning him to communicate solely in French so that the enemy would not understand. The man replied that the soldiers who had attacked their flanks that morning had regrouped and were attacking again. De Salaberry told him to draw the fight to the riverbank. When the Americans reached the river, they were met by more Voltigeurs and a barrage of fire. They hastily retreated back into the forest.

Hampton, outsmarted by his enemy once more, ordered a general withdrawal. In the haste to retreat, the American dead and wounded were left in the ravines. De Salaberry had the American wounded taken to a nearby field hospital, along with his own wounded.

Following the American retreat, de Salaberry's men immediately set to work repairing the battlements. They thought the Americans would be back. De Salaberry expected only to gain some time with his bluffs. He had not realized that he had won a decisive and complete victory against the Americans.

De Salaberry and his men spent the next eight days huddled against the abatis while a storm raged around them. They waited for an enemy that would never return. Exposed to the elements, they were utterly miserable. One of the Voltigeurs wrote, "We suffered so much from…foul weather that some of our men fell sick every day. I now know that a man could endure without dying more pain and hell than a dog. There were many things that I could tell you easier than I could write them, but you would be convinced by this affair that Canadians know how to fight."

The Battle of Chrysler's Farm
While General Hampton was leading his troops back to the border, the other arm of the American invasion force, 7000 men strong, was making its way up the St. Lawrence River in hundreds of light river boats. The flotilla made slow progress. From the Canadian side of the river, they were bombarded by cannon fire. Their commander, General Wilkinson, was sick and in no state to rally his troops. It seemed the soldiers were not in a hurry to go anywhere. It took eight days to cover 130 kilometres.

Charles-Michel de Salaberry

Along the way, the American flotilla stopped to interrogate farmers on both sides of the border, hoping to get intelligence about the British and Canadian forces. The soldiers looted the homes and property of Canadian civilians. This behaviour earned them the lasting enmity of the local population. When the Americans interrogated them, the Canadians fed them a series of outrageous tales that magnified the strength of everything from the rapids ahead to the size of the army they would face. This time, it was the civilians who tricked the Americans into believing they were up against a huge army.

Finally, on November 11, 1813, the American force reached a farm (near the present day town of Long Sault, Ontario) owned by a man named John Chrysler. They knew they could go no farther by boat until they had disabled the cannons that were still firing at them from the Canadian side of the river. The dangerous Long Sault rapids were ahead, and they could not hope to navigate them while under fire.

The Canadians and British, however, had expected the Americans to stop at Chrysler's farm. They told the Chrysler family to hide in their cellar, and then positioned their troops in the surrounding fields. There were units of British regulars, Native warriors, and the Voltigeurs. (Once de Salaberry had finally realized there would be no more action on the Chateauguay, he had led his men to the next battle.)

As always, the defending army was vastly outnumbered. Therefore, they scattered in small groups: a unit of Voltigeurs in the woods, a unit of Mohawks in a cornfield, and a unit of British regulars beyond the barns. Everywhere the Americans looked, they could see the enemy.

The Americans had already received word of Hampton's demoralizing defeat. His troops would not be joining the attack on Montreal, after all. When they saw the troops at Chrysler's farm, they realized they would have to engage them. Wilkinson, still too ill to leave his bed, ordered his junior officer to engage the British in a staid military fashion, fighting first one unit and then the next.

The officer followed his orders. The effects were debilitating. The Americans were continually harassed. Just as they appeared to dispatch one unit of the enemy, another stood up to engage. Finally, Wilkinson called the retreat. The exhausted soldiers willingly piled into their boats and retreated across the river to the American side. The attack on Montreal was a rout.

After the twin battles of Chrysler's Farm and Chateauguay, Prevost attempted to take credit for the Chateauguay victory, even though he had not arrived until the battle was all but over. In his official correspondence, he barely mentioned de Salaberry and the Voltigeurs, other than to claim that they served as the advance force for the British.

Of course, there were many witnesses to the Battle of Chateauguay, and they wanted the truth to be known. Accurate accounts of the battle appeared in the *Montreal Gazette*. Even de Salaberry, normally reticent about his achievements, was angry enough to send his own accounts of the battle back to the high command in Britain.

As it turned out, the high command had not been fooled by Prevost's claims. The legislature in Lower Canada congratulated de Salaberry on his victory and a representative of the Prince Regent made special mention of de Salaberry and the Voltigeurs in his remarks about the battle.

De Salaberry was too busy to bother himself much over Prevost's fiction. His men were exhausted; they had been on the move since early September and needed some rest. Late in November, Prevost ordered them to stage a hopeless raid on the American encampment at Four Corners, New York, the encampment where they had almost been annihilated two months earlier.

It seemed like a pointless endeavour, but de Salaberry dutifully led 300 of his men back to Four

Corners. It was cold and raining. After a miserable night in a makeshift camp, the men awoke covered in frost. They also awoke to the news that one of their scouts was missing. They reasoned he had probably been captured while reconnoitring the enemy camp. The scout who did return reported that a large contingent of Americans was waiting for them with heavy gun support. De Salaberry knew when to quit. He withdrew.

Plagued by rheumatism and fevers from his long military service, de Salaberry considered retirement. But in January 1814, he received orders to head off a possible American attack on Coteau du Lac. He hastily called up 600 Voltigeurs and some of the 49th Regiment. They marched the 60 kilometres to Coteau du Lac, losing two dozen men to frostbite along the way. When they got there, they realized it was a false alarm. There were no Americans, and no impending attack. De Salaberry returned to Montreal in February, ill and disillusioned.

When he was offered a lateral transfer that would take him out of direct fighting, de Salaberry accepted. But when an American force again massed along the border of Lower Canada, he was tempted back into active service. Together, he and his Voltigeurs defeated the invasion force.

By this time, de Salaberry had definitely had enough of military service. Now 36, he had been at war for more than half of his life. He was a married man and wanted to enjoy the pleasures of a more peaceful, domesticated life. He sent an official letter to the Duke of Kent, requesting leave to retire. His mentor did not process his request. A peace was being negotiated and the duke felt the war would soon be over. If de Salaberry could hold out for a few more months, he would be able to retire with the half-pay that was due to all officers who served the entire length of the war. De Salaberry stayed the course.

As the war drew to a close, Charles-Michel de Salaberry received accolades from his men, his generals, and his country. In 1818, he was appointed to the legislative council of Lower Canada. Years later, when most British civilians had forgotten the War of 1812, he was made a Companion of the Order of Bath.

Chapter 5
1812 – 1814
William Hamilton
Merritt

There are certain people who have the fortune, or occasionally the misfortune, to serve as witnesses to some of the most amazing events in human history. William Hamilton Merritt was just such a man. As a militiaman serving in his father's unit, and later at the head of his own elite troop of militia Dragoons, William was both a witness to — and participant in — most of the major battles of the War of 1812.

Like his father before him, William Merritt was

fiercely loyal. His father had fought for the British in the American War of Independence and afterwards moved to Canada as a United Empire Loyalist. William's loyalties belonged solely to Canada.

He had been born in Twelve Mile Creek, a small community at the northern end of the Niagara Peninsula, about 20 kilometres west of Fort George and the American border. The Niagara Peninsula was home, and he would protect it fiercely.

The Horrors of War
By the age of 20, William Merritt had already fought alongside Brock at Queenston, and with Fitzgibbon at Stoney Creek and Beaver Dams. The young man had no illusions about war.

The constant warfare was having a devastating effect on everyone in the region. On July 8, 1813, Merritt took part in a particularly violent skirmish between the Mohawks and Americans. Fighting alongside the Mohawks was a 13-year-old boy named John Lawe. His older brother had been killed in an earlier battle and his father had been wounded and taken prisoner. The boy's desire for revenge overwhelmed him. Long after the battle was officially over, he was still stumbling around the field in a state of shock, searching for the enemy. Eventually, his mother came to find him and carried the exhausted lad home in her arms.

William was disgusted with the British whenever they temporarily retreated from the Niagara Peninsula. He felt they were abandoning the settlers on the frontier, especially the Loyalists, who would pay the biggest price when the Americans swarmed over the border. Like Fitzgibbon, William was angry about the enemy's harassment of the civilians and swore to do something about it. Even during the periods when the militia had been disbanded, William and his fellow Dragoons galloped around the countryside, harassing the enemy. They clashed frequently with the hated Chapin and his guerrillas.

But, as angry as he was with the Americans, it was the actions of a fellow Canadian that appalled him most.

The Hunt for A Traitor

Joseph Willcocks was a man with a grudge against the British. Although he had fought with Brock at Queenston, his allegiance shifted soon after. The Irish immigrant to Upper Canada hated the British and, by extension, anyone loyal to the British. He was the publisher of the *Upper Canadian Guardian*. He regularly attacked the British and Loyalists in print and was twice jailed for libel. Unfortunately for the British and those loyal to them, Willcocks also had a seat in the legislature in the town of York.

In 1813, convinced that the Americans would win the war, Willcocks turned on the people he had been elected to represent. He started by passing on snippets of military intelligence. His actions were treasonous, but not really unusual at a time when loyalties were unpredictable on both sides of the border. But mere spying was not enough for Willcocks. He became a colonel in the American army while still serving in the Upper Canadian legislature. He also managed to recruit more than 100 of his fellow Canadians to fight against the Canadians and the British.

In the fall of 1813, the Americans once more invaded the Niagara Peninsula. By December, they had taken Fort George and were also in Queenston and Chippewa, just 25 kilometres east of Twelve Mile Creek. Willcocks took the opportunity to exact a little revenge on the Loyalist communities. He and his men rode around the countryside, looting and burning the farms of his former neighbours and constituents. He arrested prominent Loyalists and sent them to prisons in the United States. In Twelve Mile Creek, Willcocks arrested an 80-year-old former town warden who was a retired militiaman — a man by the name of Thomas Merritt. Thomas was William Merritt's father.

The Americans took Thomas across the border but

released him soon after. They left the elderly man to find his own way back home as best he could. When William heard of this, he was livid. He now had a burning ambition to capture or destroy the hated traitor. In his journal, William wrote that he had taken, "many [a] long and weary ride, in the lonely hours of the night, in hope of catching Willcocks and making an example of him and all traitors."

On November 28, 1813, Willcocks and his men were in the area of Twelve Mile Creek. William was soon on their trail and was slowly closing in on them. To William's frustration, Willcocks slipped away. However, two of Willcocks's men happened upon William and his crew and mistook them for Americans; the blue uniforms the Canadians wore were similar to those of some of the American regiments. From these two men, William learned that the Americans, who were in possession of Fort George at this point, had left the fort and were heading for the British position at Burlington Heights. Apparently, Willcocks and his men were acting as scouts ahead of the main force.

William chased after the traitor, and a dangerous cat and mouse game ensued. After several close calls, Willcocks escaped and returned to the main force to report to his American commander. Willcocks drastically inflated the size of the British force in the area. He reasoned the Americans would give him more leeway to interrogate and arrest British sympathisers if they thought the British forces were a real threat. The Americans, thinking they could not run the British out of Burlington Heights after all, abandoned their foray and began marching back to Fort George.

William and his commander, Colonel Murray, wanted to pursue the Americans; both men believed they could defeat their enemies while they were outside the safety of the fort. Unfortunately, they were under strict orders not to follow the retreating Americans beyond Twelve Mile Creek. It was a bitter blow.

William was also very worried about his father, who was still making his way home. He found out that Thomas had reached Shipman's Corners, a no man's land between the British and American positions. William asked for permission to leave Twelve Mile Creek on the pretext of rounding up American spies. He then went directly to Shipman's Corners and brought his father home to safety.

During this foray, he saw numerous American scouts. He thought they were probably trying to evaluate the strength of the forces in Twelve Mile Creek before deciding their next move. So as soon as he got back home, he called up the militia and told them to assemble in the town centre. Every available man and boy answered the call. When the American scouts saw the huge crowd, they were convinced it was an advance party and that the entire British and Canadian force would soon follow. That, of course, was patently untrue. At that time, the British had no intention of advancing from their position at Burlington Heights. However, this deceptive show of force was enough to persuade the commander at Fort George, Brigadier General George McClure, that he should abandon the peninsula altogether.

McClure made plans to withdraw across the Niagara River to the relative safety of their own Fort Niagara. Willcocks was furious. He had cast his lot in with the enemy and believed an American victory was within easy reach.

The Americans decided to destroy Fort George to prevent it from falling into the hands of the British. Willcocks asked McClure for permission to burn the nearby town of Newark before they burned the fort. He argued that this would prevent the inhabitants from offering shelter or sustenance to British soldiers.

Newark on Fire!
At dusk on December 10, 1813, Willcocks and his men, accompanied by a few American militiamen, rode into the town of Newark. The townspeople were warned to take what they could from their homes and leave. It had

been snowing all day and it was bitterly cold.

Willcocks started the burn at the home of an old political foe, a Loyalist by the name of William Dickson who had already been arrested. Willcocks carried the firebrand himself. He went upstairs to find the elderly Mrs. Dickson in bed. She was too ill to walk, so he ordered two of his men to carry her outside. The men wrapped the old woman in blankets and set her in a snowdrift. She watched in anguish as Willcocks burned her home to the ground.

There were other, equally horrific stories from that night. One young widow with three small children was turned out of her home with nothing but a few coins. After Willcocks's men plundered and torched her home, they took her money as well. In all, 400 women, children, and elderly men were turned out into the snow that night.

William had been on an assignment in Beaver Dams that day with Colonel Murray. As they were making their way back home, they saw the eerie orange glow of the fires in Newark. They guessed what had happened and raced to the scene. But they were already too late.

Of all the horrifying scenes William had witnessed during this war, this was the worst. All that was left of Newark were glowing embers and charred buildings. Of the 150 homes in the town, only one remained standing.

The townspeople had crowded into every room until the house could hold no more. Those left outside huddled in the drifts and beneath makeshift shelters. Some, terrified there might be more attacks, had stumbled off into the freezing night to seek shelter at outlying farms.

The streets were scattered with the remnants of a once prosperous town. Furniture, clothing, dishes, and personal treasures were everywhere, all abandoned by people too cold to carry them. The next morning, William and his men found the frozen bodies of the women and children who had been seeking shelter outside the town. They had lost their way in the blackness of the night. As many as 100 women and children had perished that night in Newark — Willcocks had certainly had his revenge. Soldiers and civilians were equally horrified at this atrocity. The burning of Newark, more than any other action in the war, united the Canadian and British troops and the civilians.

Vengeance for Newark
William was enraged. And he was not alone. The British and Canadian troops swore vengeance, and Colonel Murray was so furious that he ordered his troops to Fort George that very night, ignoring the direct orders of General Vincent not to advance.

As the British and Canadian troops galloped

towards the fort, most of the American troops, along with the traitor Willcocks, were already retreating across the border. Colonel Murray and his men captured the few remaining Americans who were still at Fort George, and then secured the fort. Neither Murray nor William was ever chastised for disobeying orders that night — the horror of Newark was too great.

Ten days later, on December 20, 1813, the reprisals began. William and his Dragoons had commandeered anything that could float. They were preparing to follow the Americans across the icy river and attack them at Fort Niagara. It had taken the Dragoons several long days and nights of toiling in the bitter cold to secure all the boats. On the night of the attack, exhausted and gripped by fever, William collapsed. He was not able to participate in the invasion he had so much wanted to be part of. It was another blow for the young man.

The American fort was heavily defended and no easy target, but it faltered quickly under the vengeful Canadian and British assault. The officers had a difficult time controlling their soldiers' bloodlust, and more than one American soldier lost his life in a private battle to avenge those lost at Newark.

Within days, the American side of the Niagara, from Fort Niagara to Buffalo, New York, was a charred ruin. In the town of Buffalo, only three buildings were left standing when the raid was over. There were atrocities committed by the Canadians and British in those battles, too. American families lost their homes and possessions. Some lost their lives to Native tomahawks. No one, it seemed, felt the need to curb the warriors' desire for vengeance anymore. The war had taken a very ugly turn.

The Americans, however, did not blame the British, the Canadians, or even the Native warriors. They held their own man, George McClure, responsible. He had allowed the burning of Newark and fuelled this spate of vengeful attacks. He was taunted and threatened on the streets of Buffalo and was soon relieved of his command.

Finally, after the many horrors during the winter of 1813, it was too cold to fight any longer. The desire for vengeance had, at long last, been exhausted. The British and Canadian soldiers retreated to their side of the Niagara River to wait for the spring thaw.

The next move was from the Americans. On July 3, 1814, in sore need of a victory, and with their border in ruins, the Americans captured Fort Erie at the southern end of the Niagara Peninsula. Then they marched towards Fort Chippewa, 10 kilometres to the north, reaching it the next day. While the troops were marching, William was having a celebratory dinner with his parents at Twelve Mile Creek. He had just turned 21. However, as soon as he heard the news, William dashed off to join the other reinforcements racing to join the battle.

Next day, July 5, the British commander at Fort Chippewa, Major General Phineas Riall, watched the Americans approach. The American soldiers were wearing grey uniforms. The militia wore this colour, so Riall thought he was facing a unit of raw militia recruits. He confidently ordered a full frontal assault, believing the militia would turn tail and run. But these soldiers did not run. Riall and his men were actually facing an entire army of hardened, well-trained career soldiers. Apparently, the Americans had run out of the blue wool used to make uniforms for the regular troops, so they had used the grey instead.

Near the close of battle, while his men were in retreat, Riall desperately charged at the Americans with only his aide at his side. He turned back only when the aide was wounded. By the time the reinforcements arrived, the battle was already over.

The British retreated to the village, where their cannons were in place. The Americans could see it would be difficult to breach that defence, so decided not to pursue the remnants of Riall's army. That night, the houses of Chippewa were filled with wounded and dying soldiers. It was a night the villagers would never forget.

Neither the British nor the Canadians were yet willing to give up the field. The British withdrew to Fort George, while the Americans camped on Queenston Heights and waited for reinforcements to arrive by ship. However, the commander of the reinforcements was sick with fever and refused to let his ships sail without him. So the Americans at Queenston continued their wait. They were becoming increasingly restless.

William Merritt spent most of the next month skirmishing with the Americans. The Niagara Peninsula was once more under siege, and civilians suffered for it. Willcocks and his band of traitors were riding again. They raided village after village, plundering and forcing the population to flee to the safety of the British forts.

But Willcocks's men were not the only ones raiding. A small group of the American soldiers still cooped up at Queenston Heights needed an outlet for their frustration. They rode to the village of St. David's and easily drove back the few British soldiers guarding the villagers. The Americans looted and burned. When William and his men arrived to help relieve the beleaguered British soldiers, 40 homes had already been destroyed. Nothing could be done to undo the wrong, but the American commanders made some amends by disciplining the soldiers responsible for the destruction of

St. David's. The soldiers were reprimanded and immediately dismissed from service.

Lundy's Lane
On July 23, 1814, the Americans received word that the reinforcements they had been waiting for would not be coming. The British and Canadians however, had been getting more reinforcements almost daily. The next day, the American commander retreated to Chippewa in order to re-supply his troops. From there, he planned to attack Burlington Heights. In the meantime, the British and Canadians had mobilized. They marched to Lundy's Lane, where Riall had sent William, along with several other officers, to scout the American positions.

On July 25, the American commander sent out a brigade of 1200 men to search the same area for enemy troops. The brigade was led by Colonel Winfield Scott, an impetuous young man. On that same day, while searching the countryside, William and his men stopped for refreshments at a tavern owned by a widow named Deborah Wilson. The Widow Wilson was well known to both armies. She indiscriminately dished out both liquor and information to the patrons seated at her wooden tables, be they British, Canadian, or American.

William and his men were just about to sit down when a scout rushed in to tell them the Americans were on their way. The Canadians raced outside and jumped on their horses. As the American brigade approached, they began firing. William paused for a second and cheekily waved to them before galloping off.

Scott searched the tavern, but no soldiers were found. Then he questioned the Widow Wilson. She quickly told Scott what William had told her: Major General Riall was waiting at a nearby farm with 1100 men. She was right; Riall was nearby, but he was accompanied by almost three times that many soldiers.

Scott was anxious to fight and did not want to wait for reinforcements. Instead, he blindly rushed in to engage the enemy. He had 1200 men, so he reasoned the 1100 men with Riall should not prove to be a problem.

The battle raged all afternoon and into the night. The two armies were often only metres apart. They could easily see the faces of their enemies. Yet still they fought on, firing volley after volley. The battle was fought, wrote one soldier, "with a desperation verging on madness."

Joseph Willcocks was at the battle. He was afraid of being captured, for he knew he would be hanged as a traitor. The Upper Canadian government had already tried and found him guilty in absentia. Around midnight, fearing the battle would be lost, he disappeared into the darkness.

In the blackness of that night, horrific mistakes were made. Troops fired on themselves. Men engaged in hand-to-hand combat only to discover that the man they grappled with was one of their own.

At one point, a group of American soldiers fought their way through the woods and surrounded Riall. He was taken prisoner, but his men fought on. William, who had joined the battle as soon as the firing had started, attempted a rescue. But he was captured as well.

By morning, the men of both sides were too exhausted to continue; the battle was finally over. The Americans had quit the field, leaving their wounded and heavy artillery behind in their haste. The British were in no condition to follow the retreating Americans. The battlefield was littered with hundreds of bodies. Those who were there said it was difficult to distinguish the dead from those who had merely fallen into an exhausted sleep. It took all morning to separate the wounded from the dead. The British and Canadian dead were buried in a mass grave, and the American dead were burnt in a giant funeral pyre.

In their hasty retreat back to Fort Erie, the Americans were forced to dump wagonloads of supplies and arms in order to use the wagons to transport the wounded. William Merritt was an unwilling participant in that retreat. The Americans took him and their other prisoners with them to jails in the United States.

Lundy's Lane was one of the bloodiest battles of the war. The British and Canadians suffered 880 men wounded, captured, or killed. The Americans suffered a similar number of casualties. Both sides claimed victory. Although the Americans had abandoned the field, the battle did much to prop up the flagging American enthusiasm for the war.

The horrors of that day were recorded by a young British surgeon named William "Tiger" Dunlop. The only surgeon on the battlefield, he had to tend 220 wounded men. He recounted in his journal the story of one woman who entered the makeshift surgery. She was searching for her elderly husband. When she finally found him, she saw that he had been mortally wounded. The woman sank down beside her husband and cried. Then, momentarily stunned by the devastation surrounding her, she took her dying husband's head on her lap and cried out, "O that the King and the President were both here this moment to see the misery their quarrels lead to — they surely would never go to war without a cause that they could give as a reason to God at the last day, for thus destroying the creatures that He had made in his own image?"

William Hamilton Merritt

Whimpers of War

At the end of July, the Americans entrenched in Fort Erie were preparing for yet another invasion. But their plans were interrupted. On August 15, 1814, the British attacked the fort. The British and Canadians won a decisive victory at the battle and finally drove the Americans back across the border. William Merritt's friends and family at Twelve Mile Creek, and the other Niagara villagers, had endured their last battle. They had also endured their last torment from Joseph Willcocks. The hated traitor had been killed at the battle. Imprisoned in the United States, William cheered when he heard the news.

On August 25, 1814, the Canadians and British swarmed into the navel base at Bladensburg, New York, and easily disarmed the militia guarding this entrance to Washington. By nightfall, the capitol itself had been set afire. Public buildings were looted and documents littered the city streets.

While that fire was ravaging the American capital, representatives of Britain and America were meeting in the Belgian town of Ghent to discuss possible terms for peace. As the politicians continued their negotiations, soldiers were fighting more battles on land, lakes, and sea.

The Canadians and British won a series of naval victories on Lake Champlain. Both the Americans and the British were heavily engaged in a race to build bigger and better ships. The war with Napoleon was at an end and 16,000 battle-hardened troops had recently arrived in Canada to help end the war.

In September, Governor Prevost began a march on Plattsburgh, New York. He led the largest army the British had fielded to date. His land attack was to have occurred simultaneously with a British naval attack on Plattsburgh Bay. However, Prevost was in a hurry. He put pressure on the naval commanders to engage. They were not ready, but they reluctantly followed his commands. The battle was over in just over two hours — the British surrendered. It was the first time they had been defeated at sea.

When Prevost heard that the navy had been defeated, he called a retreat, even though his troops outnumbered the enemy three to one. His commanders were devastated and tried to argue with him. But he refused to listen. The army retreated. They were, it was said, halfway to the Canadian border before the Americans even realized they were gone.

On January 8, 1815, British and Canadian troops attacked the port of New Orleans, Louisiana. The Americans won a stunning victory. The toll for the British and Americans was 2000 dead or wounded.

A victory of this magnitude, in other circumstances, might have won the war for the Americans. In fact, for a few weeks after the battle, the American populace believed the war was theirs. But it had all been for naught. Two weeks before the battle, on December 24, 1814, the negotiators in Ghent had signed a treaty officially ending the war.

When word of the peace finally reached North America in February of 1815, William Merritt was at last allowed to go back home to Twelve Mile Creek. He married and raised a family in the little town he loved. An enterprising man, he was one of the visionaries who proposed the creation of the Welland Canal just a few years after the end of the war. He also took part in convincing the American and Canadian governments to build a bridge across the Niagara River, the former border between the two countries.

Epilogue

Journal Entry
Niagara Falls, Ontario
July 2003

Today I visited Lundy's Lane, the place where my great-grandfather, James Williams, fought his last battle in the War of 1812. As I watch cars race back and forth between Canada and the United States on the aptly named Peace Bridge, it's difficult to believe that the two countries once fought a vicious war over this land.

My great-grandfather survived that war, but thousands didn't. The British suffered more than 5000 dead and wounded; the American toll was close to 7000. No one bothered to keep track of how many Canadian militiamen fell on the battlefields, or of how many Native people lost their lives. And there are no records of how many militiamen died from exposure or diseases. The best guess is that it was three to four times as many as died from their wounds.

What a waste of life! So many people lost so much.

Epilogue

But the biggest losers were the Native peoples. They were hardly mentioned in the Treaty of Ghent, and they didn't receive any of the protection and support promised them by the British. The Treaty didn't address the issue of impressments, either. And this was supposed to be the reason the Americans declared war in the first place! It was a moot point, anyway. Once the war with Napoleon was over, the British didn't need to impress anyone into their navy.

There wasn't even a clear winner in this war. Still, my great-grandfather believed he'd done the right thing by defending Canada. He once told my grandfather that British colonials died on the battlefields in the war, but Canadians were born in their place.

It was true. If the war accomplished anything, it was the emergence of a fierce, new Canadian patriotism. The war laid the foundations for unifying these British colonies into the country that became Canada in 1867.

I think my great-grandfather would be proud of the nation we have become. We've built a strong country, maintained our friendship with the British, and forged a strong relationship with the United States. Ours is the longest undefended border in the world.

Emily Williams Montgomery

War of 1812 Chronology

Battle of Tippecanoe . . . . November 7, 1811
U.S. Declaration of War . . . . June 19, 1812
Capture of the *Cuyahoga Packet* . . . . June 21, 1812
Hull occupies Sandwich . . . . July 12, 1812
Fort Michilimackinac taken . . . . July 17, 1812
Battle of Brownstown . . . . August 5, 1812
Capture of Fort Detroit . . . . August 16, 1812
Battle of Queenston Heights . . . . October 13, 1812
Battle of La Colle . . . . November 27, 1812
The River Raisin Massacre . . . . January 19, 1813
Battle of Stoney Creek . . . . June 6, 1813
Battle of Beaver Dams . . . . June 24, 1813
Battle of Lake Erie . . . . September 10, 1813
Battle of the Thames (Moraviantown) . . . October 5, 1813
Battle of Chateauguay . . . . October 25, 1813
Battle of Chrysler's Farms . . . . November 11, 1813
Burning of Newark . . . . December 10, 1813
Burning of the U.S. Niagara begins . . . . . December 20, 1813
Battle at Chippewa . . . . July 5, 1814
Battle of Lundy's Lane . . . . July 25, 1814
Battle of Fort Erie . . . . August 15, 1814
Washington Burns . . . . August 24, 1814
Treaty of Ghent . . . . December 24, 1814
Battle of New Orleans . . . . January 8, 1815

Bibliography

Berton, Pierre. *Flames Across the Border 1812-1813*. Toronto: McClelland and Stewart, 1981.

Berton, Pierre. *The Invasion of Canada 1812-1813*. Toronto: McClelland and Stewart, 1980.

Elliot, James. *Billy Green and the Battle of Stoney Creek, June 6, 1813*. Stoney Creek: Battlefield House Museum.

Hitsman, Mackay J. *The Incredible War of 1812: A Military History*. Toronto: Robert Brass Studio, 1999.

Mackenzie, Ruth. *James Fitzgibbon: Defender of Upper Canada*. Toronto: Dundurn Press, 1983.

Mackenzie, Ruth. *Laura Secord: The Legend and the Lady*. Toronto: McClelland and Stewart, 1971.

McLeod, Carol. *Legendary Canadian Women*. Nova Scotia: Lancelot Press, 1983.

Bibliography

Ryerson, Edgerton. *Loyalists of America and Their Times.* Toronto: 1880. The Historical Memorandum of Amelia Ryerse.

Stanley, George. *The War of 1812: Land Operations.* Toronto: Macmillan of Canada, 1983.

Sugden, John. *Tecumseh : a life.* New York: H. Holt, 1998.

Sutherland, Stewart, Ed. *A desire of serving and defending my country : the War of 1812 journals of William Hamilton Merritt.* Toronto: Iser Publications, 2001.

Wohler, Patrick J. *Charles de Salaberry: Soldier of the Empire, Defender of Quebec.* Toronto: Dundurn Press, 1984.

Films
Canada: A People's History. Episode 5: A Question of Loyalties. Canadian Broadcasting Corporation. http://www.cbc.ca/homevideo/Drama/history.htm

The War of 1812. Galafilms. Four Part Documentary Directed By Robert McKenna. www.galafilm.com/1812

Acknowledgments

I would like to recognize the National Archives of Canada, Pierre Berton's *The Invasion of Canada* and *Flames Across the Border* and Patrick Wohler's book on Charles de Salaberry as sources for the quotes used in this book.

Thank you to my editor, Pat Kozak, for her work and help.

I also want to thank my husband Alex and my history-loving daughters — Danielle, Kathleen, Alexandria, Emily, and Laura — for their unstinting support, and my parents, Terry and Linda Burke, for encouraging my own interest in history.

Finally, thank you to Ruth and Dan Crump for their interest and encouragement, and for the numerous tours of the areas known to Tecumseh and Brock as Forts Amherstberg and Detroit.

Photo Credits

About the Author

Jennifer Crump is a freelance journalist and author whose work has appeared in numerous North American magazines, including *Reader's Digest, Canadian Geographic,* and *Today's Parent.* She is also the author of a guidebook on the city of Toronto. When she's not writing, she is reading. History, particularly Canadian history, is a long-time passion. A former resident of the southern part of Upper Canada, Jennifer now lives with her family in the northern part of the province.

AMAZING STORIES™

DINOSAUR HUNTERS

Uncovering the Hidden Remains
of Canada's Ancient Giants

HISTORY/BIOGRAPHY

by Lisa Murphy-Lamb

Dinosaur Hunters
ISBN 1-55153-982-9

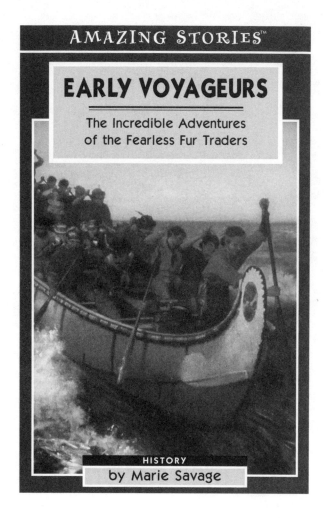
Early Voyageurs
ISBN 1-55153-970-5

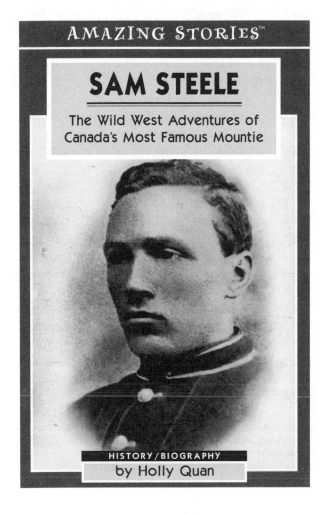

AMAZING STORIES™

SAM STEELE

The Wild West Adventures of
Canada's Most Famous Mountie

HISTORY/BIOGRAPHY
by Holly Quan

Sam Steele
ISBN 1-55153-997-7

OTHER AMAZING STORIES

These titles are available wherever you buy books. If you have trouble finding the book you want, call the Altitude order desk at 1-800-957-6888, e-mail your request to: orderdesk@altitudepublishing.com or visit our Web site at www.amazingstories.ca

All titles retail for $9.95 Cdn or $7.95 US. (Prices subject to change.)

New AMAZING STORIES titles are published every month. If you would like more information, e-mail your name and mailing address to: amazingstories@altitudepublishing.com.